SUPERWORDPOWER

SuperWordPower

Eugene Ehrlich

A Hudson Group Book

PERENNIAL LIBRARY

Harper & Row, Publishers, New York

Cambridge, Philadelphia, San Francisco, London
Mexico City, São Paulo, Singapore, Sydney

FIRST EDITION

Designed by Lorraine Mullaney

Library of Congress Cataloging-in-Publication Data

Ehrlich, Eugene H.
  SuperWordPower.

  "A Hudson Group book."
  Includes index.
  1. Vocabulary—Problems, exercises, etc.   I. Title.   II. Title: Super word power.
PE1449.E37   1988   428.1'076   88-45556
ISBN 0-06-096314-X

---

89   90   91   92   93   DT/FG   10   9   8   7   6   5   4   3   2   1

For Margie and Alice

CONTENTS

PREFACE

Who can resist the intellectual challenge posed by a truly demanding vocabulary test, especially when the test is self-administered and self-scored? Finding out how extensive one's vocabulary is provides a measure of satisfaction plus a road map for future growth of vocabulary. So if you relish a challenge and are interested in learning new words, *SuperWordPower* represents an excellent opportunity to enrich your vocabulary further by taking and scoring a series of one hundred multiple-choice tests.

Learning all the words in *SuperWordPower* will increase your ability to read difficult texts without continual reference to an unabridged dictionary and will increase your ability to write precisely and colorfully. Above all, *SuperWordPower* offers the pure pleasure of adding to your store of useful knowledge.

The twelve hundred SuperWordPower entries in this book were selected from published works written for intelligent and well-informed adults. As a result, even if your present vocabulary is well above average, the one hundred SuperWordPower tests in this book will challenge your knowledge. Those whose store of words is not already above average may find other vocabulary books more rewarding.

Each SuperWordPower test presents ten words to be defined, and these are followed by two bonus words intended for those whose vocabularies are outstandingly rich. For your convenience, answers for all the SuperWordPower tests are supplied at the end of Test One Hundred.

Each of the one hundred tests begins with words known to most mature readers. As a test progresses, the challenge increases, and the final questions in each test are quite difficult. The first ten test words are presented in sentences intended to illustrate proper word usage. At the same time, care has been taken not to reveal the correct definitions of the words through contextual clues. This increases the difficulty of the tests somewhat, but it also adds to their validity.

The exceptionally difficult bonus words are intended to challenge even those who can define many relatively rare words. For this reason, the eleventh and twelfth words in each test have been dubbed *zingers,* conveying the sense that they are words known to few people. To make these last two questions even more challenging, *zingers* are presented without benefit of illustrative sentences.

Some advice to keep in mind when working your way through *SuperWordPower:* (1) Test words sometimes are defined in unfamiliar senses, so you should examine all the suggested answers carefully before responding to a test question. (2) After completing a test and checking your answers, it is advisable to consult an unabridged dictionary to find all meanings of words you wish to learn.

Acquiring **SuperWordPower**

You may recall a wonderful time in your life when a single encounter with a new word was enough to make the word yours forever. Reading the word in a context that made the meaning clear, hearing it defined, or reading the definition in a dictionary just once would do the trick. Those were the days.

There came a time in your intellectual development when you felt the need to make lists of new words so that one day you could look them up and learn them. Much of the time you mislaid the lists or never found the right opportunity for spending the required hours with your dictionary. At times of crisis, for example in the months before taking a scholastic aptitude test, you may have tried to learn great numbers of difficult words by saying the words and their definitions to yourself over and over again. This repetitive drill may have achieved its purpose—you did well in your tests—but did you actually learn many of the words well enough so that you knew what they meant a few weeks or months after the test? If your experience was that of most people who have tried to cram in this way, not likely.

If the ability to learn new words easily appears to have vanished, you are not alone. As adults acquire more and more information and more and more experience, they typically find that vocabulary-building, an exercise in abstract learning, demands sustained effort. Ask yourself how many times you have gone back to a dictionary for the second, third, fourth time or more for help with a word you have wrestled with before.

The sad fact is that even though you may resolve to learn a definition so you won't have to use your dictionary yet again for that same word, mere resolve usually proves fruitless. Soon enough, there you are at your dictionary for yet one more consultation. The hopelessness of reading a definition over and over again in widely separated sessions with a dictionary makes it clear that something else must be done to fix words and their meanings in your memory.

If you wish to go on increasing the strength and versatility of the vocabulary you need for reading, writing, and speaking, it is helpful to use a systematic approach to learning new words. The time it takes to make new words your own will be insignificant when measured against the bother of looking up the same words repeatedly. With an effective learning procedure, you will find that the next time you encounter a difficult word you have studied, its meaning will be immediately apparent. And you will be able to use the word readily and naturally in your writing and speech.

Any effective vocabulary-building system must be based on repeated recitation and test. There is no need to attend a course in vocabulary development to become serious about improving your knowledge of words. Even though you may take pleasure in going to class and indeed benefit from the discipline of regular assignments and recitations, you probably now have everything you need to do the job on your own.

The materials involved in one highly successful system consist of a source of words to be learned, a desk dictionary, and a supply of slips of paper or index cards.

First a word on the source of vocabulary to be learned. Best of all is a collection of books you have always intended to read. Books that attract intelligent adults inevitably employ language that may challenge your present knowledge. Because you have a desire to read the books, you will find that the vocabulary will also be of interest to you.

If your present desk dictionary meets your needs in clarity and comprehensiveness, you will not have to look elsewhere. If you find, however, that your dictionary often fails to include words you need to understand, then you should replace it. The problem may be that your dictionary is out of date or does not cover fields of interest special to you. Before you buy a new dictionary, spend time in a bookstore looking up the same words in each of the dictionaries offered for sale. See how the dictionaries define those words. When you find that a particular dictionary has the words you want and provides clear definitions, you have found your new dictionary.

Finally, you will need slips of paper or cards. A convenient size is approximately three inches by five inches. Slips are inexpensive to come by in pad form but are not as easy to handle as index cards, which may be purchased in packets of fifty or one hundred.

Now you have everything you need to launch an effective program of vocabulary-building. Let us assume that you are reading a book and have near at hand a batch of cards and your desk dictionary. In your reading you encounter the word *provenance* in the following sentence: "The provenance of the painting has never been determined." On one side of a card, write *provenance*, the word you wish to learn.

provenance

On the back of the card, write the sentence in which the word appeared.

The provenance of the painting has
never been determined.

Consult your dictionary to find the meaning of the word. Since many words are defined in more than one way, be certain that the dictionary definition you find is one that fits the use of the word in the sentence in which you found it. The *Random House Dictionary of the English Language* supplies the following definition of *provenance:* "place or source of origin." You are ready to add to the back of your card.

The provenance of the painting has
never been determined.

place or source of origin

Now you have a card that will enable you to test your learning of the definition of *provenance* enough times to be absolutely certain of what the word means and how it is used.

It is especially helpful to write the card yourself. Writing by hand gives you contact with the word, and many people find this contact useful in learning. Another reason is that the act of creating a card starts you on the road to effective learning, and so it will for every word you wish to learn and every card you make.

Let us count up the chances you have already had for learning a word such as *provenance* merely by creating the card. (1) You have read the word in a book. (2) You have written it on a card. (3) You have written the sentence in which it appeared. (4) You have looked the word up in your dictionary. (5) You have written a definition on your card. Thus, you have already had five encounters with the word.

In many cases, once you have reached this stage, you will already know the word and its meaning. But this will not be true if you find many new words in a session of reading. So the process must be completed.

This is the way to do so. After you have begun to write cards, set aside time for recitation and self-test in the following manner. Read aloud the word on the front of a card. Without looking at the back of the card, recite the sentence in which you found the word. Again without looking at the back of the card, recite the definition of the word. Then look at the back of the card. If you correctly recalled both the definition and the sentence, write a checkmark on the front of the card and go on to the next card, repeating the process until you have reviewed the rest of your cards.

When you cannot recall a sentence and definition, read the word aloud along with its sentence and definition. You earn a checkmark for a card only when you can recite the sentence and definition successfully.

Study your pack of cards on alternate days to make certain that your learning of a word persists.

By the time you have awarded yourself three checkmarks on a card, you have probably made a permanent addition to your vocabulary. There is nothing magical about three checkmarks in this context. What is important is that by then you have had a total of at least eight chances to learn each word, five encounters to create a card plus three perfect recitations.

Satisfied that you know a three-checkmark word, retire its card from your growing pack of cards and file the card in alphabetical order along with other new words learned. About a month after you begin to collect your new words, launch a monthly review of your alphabetical collection, looking only at the word on the front of a card and testing your memory of its definition and sentence. You will find that you have nearly perfect recall of every word.

As time goes by, you will also find that the words you have learned recur in your reading and in conversation, and that you handle them with ease. In addition, you will find yourself able to call on your new words whenever you need them for writing or speech. You will be well on your way to SuperWordPower.

SUPERWORDPOWER

Test
<u>ONE</u>

1. Prolonged trips in outer space may yet be shown to produce **deleterious** effects on the human body.

    a. ☐ healthful

    b. ☐ mysterious

    c. ☐ unpredictable

    d. ☑ harmful

    e. ☐ organic

2. As soon as the first intermission was over, the comments of the audience made it clear that theater reviewers would characterize the play as yet another **debacle** for its author.

    a. ☐ great success

    b. ☑ complete failure

    c. ☐ step forward in a career

    d. ☐ financial success

    e. ☐ mediocre achievement

3. **Gauche** remarks came from him that night with a rapidity previously unsurpassed.

    a. ☐ tactless

    b. ☐ inappropriate

    c. ☐ vengeful

    d. ☐ unscrupulous

    e. ☐ insincere

4. You can count on being **castigated** by your supervisor if your job performance remains at its present level.

    a. ☐ recommended for promotion

    b. ☐ publicly commended

c. ☐ congratulated

d. ☐ demoted

e. ☐ severely criticized

5. As the campaign dragged into its final weeks, the candidate more and more was given to **egregious** blunders in his speeches.

a. ☐ untimely

b. ☐ outrageous

c. ☐ forgivable

d. ☐ thoughtless

e. ☐ unpreventable

6. The first characteristic that comes to mind in describing young Hazel is her **ebullience.**

a. ☐ customary apathy

b. ☐ fairness in dealing with others

c. ☐ general stubbornness

d. ☐ pervasive calm

e. ☐ enthusiastic expression of feelings

7. Just how much of their tiresome **badinage** can you take without losing patience?

a. ☐ playful repartee

b. ☐ underhanded actions

c. ☐ malicious jokes

d. ☐ sexist remarks

e. ☐ gossip

8. After many years' absence from the campus, I once again found myself playing the role of **abecedarian.**

a. ☐ teacher of freshman English

b. ☐ teacher of remedial English

c. ☐ calligrapher

d. ☐ student of the rudiments of a subject

e. ☐ stern disciplinarian

9. As each **fascicle** was made available to the public, readers became increasingly attracted to the novel.

a. ☐ division of a book published in parts

b. ☐ advance notice for a book

c. ☐ early review of a book

d. ☐ publicity before official publication of a book

e. ☐ church commentary on the worth of a book

10. Over the years that followed, Edward acquired his apparently well-deserved reputation as **flaneur** of the first rank.

a. ☐ dessert chef

b. ☐ clothing designer

c. ☐ arsonist

d. ☐ aimless person

e. ☐ connoisseur

■ *ZINGERS*

A. **janissary:** one of a group of

a. ☐ staunch opponents

b. ☐ eloquent officials

c. ☐ official emissaries

d. ☐ appointed seers

e. ☐ subservient supporters

B. **zucchetto:** a small skullcap worn by

a. ☐ a member of the clergy

b. ☐ an Italian peasant

c. ☐ a child at play

d. ☐ a member of a surgical team

e. ☐ a technician using delicate equipment

Test
TWO

1. It was clear to most of us that **kowtowing** would not resolve the bitter dispute.

a. ☐ showing fear

b. ☐ showing obsequious deference

c. ☐ showing ordinary respect

d. ☐ showing disrespect

e. ☐ showing animosity

2. His **maladroit** handling of the situation produced the expected outcome.

a. ☐ awkward

b. ☐ unpardonable

c. ☐ skillful

d. ☐ tentative

e. ☐ unjustifiable

3. We never believed or expected that his senior advisers would be **omniscient.**

a. ☐ forgetful of everything

b. ☐ completely fair to all

c. ☐ always attentive

d. ☐ capable of sufficient insight

e. ☐ possessed of complete knowledge

4. The candidate knew he had to defend himself against charges of **nepotism** made against the previous administration.

  a. ☐ misappropriation of public funds
  b. ☐ favoritism shown to relatives
  c. ☐ indecisiveness in dealing with legislators
  d. ☐ unwillingness to hear opinions of others
  e. ☐ stirring up controversy

5. Everyone did his best to placate the two factions, yet no one could prevent the inevitable **imbroglio** we all anticipated.

  a. ☐ impasse
  b. ☐ bitter altercation
  c. ☐ complete silence
  d. ☐ slight reduction in tension
  e. ☐ departure of all concerned

6. In that court, according to observers, most judges are known for the **lenity** of the sentences they hand down.

  a. ☐ fairness
  b. ☐ unmerited clemency
  c. ☐ severity
  d. ☐ evenhandedness
  e. ☐ extreme harshness

7. Experts recommend that a defective **helve** is best replaced as soon as the condition is detected.

  a. ☐ plaster cast
  b. ☐ machine part
  c. ☐ die fixture
  d. ☐ tool handle
  e. ☐ camshaft

8. One taste I shall never forget is that of highly spiced food cooked in **ghee.**

   a. ☐ virgin olive oil

   b. ☐ clarified butter

   c. ☐ vegetable oil

   d. ☐ animal fat

   e. ☐ fresh coconut milk

9. Despite the thoroughness of the commission's work, the feeling persisted that the public had gained only an **inchoate** understanding of the new tax system.

   a. ☐ confused

   b. ☐ distorted

   c. ☐ misleading

   d. ☐ superficial

   e. ☐ incomplete

10. By that time the customary **lagniappe** no longer worked its magic.

   a. ☐ excessive servility

   b. ☐ prompt service

   c. ☐ courtesy and efficiency

   d. ☐ gift of food and drink

   e. ☐ something given by way of good measure

■ *ZINGERS*

A. **adscititious:** acquired or derived from

   a. ☐ family wealth

   b. ☐ a chance encounter

   c. ☐ an external source

d. ☐   penetrating analysis

e. ☐   personal resources

B. **hapax legomenon:** a word or phrase that

a. ☐   once uttered cannot be retracted

b. ☐   derives from a classical source in unchanged form

c. ☐   is intended as the final comment on the subject being discussed

d. ☐   occurs only once in a work or once in the entire work of an author

e. ☐   once uttered cannot be challenged on factual grounds

Test
THREE

1. The quality he retained until just before death claimed him was his irrepressible **verbosity**.

a. ☐   pomposity

b. ☐   sense of humor

c. ☐   wordiness

d. ☐   clarity of thought

e. ☐   word sense

2. I admire anyone who truly can be described as having **savoir faire**.

a. ☐   knowledge of machinery

b. ☐   outstanding intelligence

c. ☐   ability to react to stress

d. ☐   social tact

e. ☐   courage and persistence

3. One of the members of the group characterized the entire afternoon's discussion as **palaver.**

   a. ☐   interesting discourse

   b. ☐   fair representation of all points of view

   c. ☐   unfair and narrow restriction of subject matter

   d. ☐   idle talk

   e. ☐   brisk and productive discussion

4. By those who did not know him well, he was perceived as a **taciturn** person.

   a. ☐   talkative

   b. ☐   trustworthy

   c. ☐   given to saying little

   d. ☐   given to moodiness

   e. ☐   inclined to bouts of depression

5. The **regimen** he encountered turned out to be more than he had bargained for.

   a. ☐   rules of the game

   b. ☐   military discipline

   c. ☐   autocratic rule

   d. ☐   military junta

   e. ☐   regulated course of training

6. Once all the pertinent facts became known, it was clear that an **odious** policy underlay all that had happened.

   a. ☐   deserving repugnance

   b. ☐   meriting close scrutiny

   c. ☐   less than praiseworthy

   d. ☐   creating offensive odors

   e. ☐   unnecessarily burdensome

7. As a condition to agreeing to the attorney's suggestion that the suit be dropped, Lois insisted on a **quid pro quo.**

    a. ☐   reduction of a lawyer's fees

    b. ☐   something in exchange for something else

    c. ☐   prompt and complete apology

    d. ☐   advice from a third party

    e. ☐   consultation with a judge

8. Most unexpectedly, the words the speaker employed were appropriate to a **panegyric** rather than to a careful examination of the political issues.

    a. ☐   savage attack

    b. ☐   reversal of previously held opinion

    c. ☐   elaborate praise

    d. ☐   all-encompassing denial of earlier claims

    e. ☐   narrow discussion

9. Some legal experts hold the opinion that the statute, as drafted, is **nugatory.**

    a. ☐   fair

    b. ☐   oppressive

    c. ☐   invalid

    d. ☐   biased

    e. ☐   enforceable

10. I was not prepared for the **mansuetude** I encountered in the powerful executive.

    a. ☐   ill-temperedness

    b. ☐   poor manners

    c. ☐   open-mindedness

   d. ☐ gentleness

   e. ☐ indecisiveness

■ *ZINGERS*

A. **afflatus:**

   a. ☐ extrasensory perception

   b. ☐ divine communication of knowledge

   c. ☐ overpowering feeling of elation

   d. ☐ pretentious attitude

   e. ☐ extreme indigestion

B. **clerihew:**

   a. ☐ a type of religious devotion

   b. ☐ a type of comic verse

   c. ☐ devotion to detail

   d. ☐ a type of religious training

   e. ☐ a technique used in dissection

Test
FOUR

1. Great men and women usually are marked by a degree of **unpretentiousness** often lacking in people of lesser accomplishment.

   a. ☐ clarity of thought

   b. ☐ modesty

   c. ☐ sincerity

   d. ☐ honesty

   e. ☐ common sense

2. The sport of fishing is thought to offer a **salubrious** way to spend one's free time.

    a. ☐ productive

    b. ☐ conducive to health

    c. ☐ useful

    d. ☐ demanding but satisfying

    e. ☐ restful

3. Most of the guests at the groom's stag party could be described as **jocund,** if not ribald.

    a. ☐ partially inebriated

    b. ☐ interested primarily in athletics

    c. ☐ marked by high spirits

    d. ☐ almost antisocial

    e. ☐ interested in food and drink

4. We look forward to Christmas Day each year, when we can watch grandfather's smiling, **rubicund** face as he opens his presents.

    a. ☐ of healthy reddish color

    b. ☐ shining with anticipation

    c. ☐ well-rounded

    d. ☐ generous

    e. ☐ benevolent

5. The most recent faculty meeting was marked by the extraordinary absence of **sententious** speeches by senior professors.

    a. ☐ excessively moralistic

    b. ☐ witty and perceptive

    c. ☐ wise but long-winded

    d. ☐ provocative and insightful

    e. ☐ intellectually challenging

6. Beyond the village lies an ancient **ossuary** that attracts much attention among the thousands who visit the site each year.

a. ☐   place for the bones of the dead

b. ☐   place for punishment of criminals

c. ☐   place for temporary storage of artifacts

d. ☐   place for contemplation of nature

e. ☐   place for studying petrified trees and plants

7. By reputation he was a person incapable of **traducing** even minor traffic laws.

a. ☐   violating

b. ☐   understanding

c. ☐   complying with

d. ☐   coping with

e. ☐   overlooking

8. He takes great delight in discussing **solecisms** found in the work of others, apparently unaware that he too is gifted in this respect.

a. ☐   expressions of excessive concern for self

b. ☐   pithy expressions

c. ☐   displays of erudition

d. ☐   errors in logical reasoning

e. ☐   ungrammatical constructions

9. Experts who attended the exhibition said that most of the paintings were **recherché.**

a. ☐   difficult to understand

b. ☐   of studied elegance

c. ☐   suitable only for collectors

d. ☐   highly sought after

e. ☐   imitative of earlier works

10. In wartime, **triage** makes sense for field hospitals that are faced with overwhelming demands on limited medical resources.

a. ☐ careful study and assignment of available nurses and physicians

b. ☐ rapid experimentation to achieve efficient treatment of all the wounded

c. ☐ analysis of costs and benefits in offering medical treatment

d. ☐ giving treatment to the most badly injured before treating others

e. ☐ employment of a system of priorities for treatment of the wounded to maximize the number of survivors

■ *ZINGERS*

A. **chrestomathy:** a selection of

a. ☐ passages from the work of an author

b. ☐ familiar literary quotations

c. ☐ moral tales and poems

d. ☐ classical wisdom

e. ☐ scholarly papers on a single topic

B. **fainéant:**

a. ☐ pretender to a throne

b. ☐ obsequious flatterer

c. ☐ habitual plagiarist

d. ☐ irresponsible idler

e. ☐ habitual imitator

Test
FIVE

1. I believe you should judge the containers primarily on whether they are sufficiently **capacious** for most of your needs.

a. ☐ well suited

b. ☐ versatile

c. ☐ of large capacity

d. ☐ reliable

e. ☐ high in quality

2. Upon entering the school building, we were struck by the **decorum** of the students.

a. ☐ correctness in behavior

b. ☐ willingness to help one another

c. ☐ interest in free exchange of ideas

d. ☐ artistic ability

e. ☐ outlandish behavior

3. His rich imagination transported him to a **seraglio** rich in ornate trappings.

a. ☐ exotic land

b. ☐ foreign quarter

c. ☐ oriental bazaar

d. ☐ watering place

e. ☐ harem of a Muslim palace

4. The candidate's **truculent** responses astounded even veteran political reporters.

a. ☐ incisive and logical

b. ☐ defiant and aggressive

c. ☐ vague and indecisive

d. ☐ disorganized and desultory

e. ☐ demeaning and self-serving

5. **Aberrant** behavior is characteristic of members of that age group.

a. ☐ aggressively hostile in manner

b. ☐ falling silent to avoid unpleasantness

c. ☐ suggesting ready agreement

d. ☐ deviating from what is normal

e. ☐ suggesting open disagreement

6. **Baksheesh** opened doors for them wherever they went.

a. ☐ expressions of politeness

b. ☐ friendly smiles

c. ☐ small gifts of money

d. ☐ awareness of local customs

e. ☐ good manners

7. Well before reaching town, they encountered the beginnings of what their guide identified as a typical **effluvium.**

a. ☐ small stream rich in aquatic life

b. ☐ unpleasant or harmful gas

c. ☐ small area sparsely covered by stunted plants and trees

d. ☐ fast-moving river

e. ☐ collection of temporary dwellings

8. The audience particularly applauded the prima ballerina's beautifully executed **cabriole.**

a. ☐ leap in which one leg is extended and the other is struck against it

b. ☐ leap through the air with both legs extended

c. ☐ graceful turn on one toe with other leg extended

d. ☐   leap upward with repeated crossing of legs

e. ☐   series of leaps across the entire stage

9. Most critics characterized the author's latest work as a **farrago** unlike anything she had previously written.

a. ☐   cynical piece

b. ☐   brilliant effort

c. ☐   insightful essay

d. ☐   thoughtless piece

e. ☐   hodgepodge

10. Her new book of photographs was helpful in explaining details of tribal **wickiups.**

a. ☐   chairs made of woven branches

b. ☐   Indian huts

c. ☐   elaborate decorations made of interlaced willow twigs

d. ☐   crude tables

e. ☐   cooking utensils

■   *ZINGERS*

A. **uncinate:**

a. ☐   related by blood

b. ☐   approximate

c. ☐   hooked

d. ☐   marked by anxiety

e. ☐   smooth

B. **fatidic:** relating to

a. ☐   prophecy

b. ☐   destiny

c. ☐   fatigue

d. ☐   stupidity

e. ☐   emptiness

Test
SIX

1. Inevitably there came a time when his **forebodings** proved impossible to contain.

   a. ☐   feelings of exultation

   b. ☐   feelings of excitement

   c. ☐   feelings that trouble is coming

   d. ☐   exaggerated fears

   e. ☐   bouts of unjustifiable optimism

2. His friends were so accustomed to his general **haplessness** that they no longer paid it any attention.

   a. ☐   unluckiness

   b. ☐   carelessness

   c. ☐   good fortune

   d. ☐   pessimism

   e. ☐   optimism

3. Those who persist in playing the role of **gadfly** may sooner or later see their efforts yield beneficial results.

   a. ☐   habitual busybody

   b. ☐   exceptionally hard worker

   c. ☐   meticulous observer

   d. ☐   careful worker

   e. ☐   persistently annoying critic

4. Mistakenly or not, by the time she reached the threshold of her greatness, her contemporaries perceived her primarily as an **iconoclast.**

    a. ☐   painter of religious figures

    b. ☐   person who attacks cherished beliefs

    c. ☐   middle-of-the-roader

    d. ☐   serious thinker

    e. ☐   misguided idealist

5. He was wont to consider himself **doyen** of the figure painters then active.

    a. ☐   most progressive member of a group

    b. ☐   best trained member of a group

    c. ☐   natural leader of a group

    d. ☐   logical choice for a position of leadership in a group

    e. ☐   senior member of a group

6. The speaker's **malapropisms** evoked laughter among most of those present, but her supporters anguished in complete silence.

    a. ☐   common errors in syntax

    b. ☐   transparent exaggerations

    c. ☐   comical confusions of words

    d. ☐   ridiculous claims

    e. ☐   unfortunate errors in pronunciation

7. Our child's **febrile** condition was ample indication that something was still wrong.

    a. ☐   nervous

    b. ☐   feverish

    c. ☐   tremulous

    d. ☐   gloomy

    e. ☐   marked by poor appetite

8. Their intention was to **extirpate** prejudice by a program of reeducation.

  a. ☐ eradicate

  b. ☐ reduce

  c. ☐ explain

  d. ☐ explore

  e. ☐ counteract

9. Despite years of use, the fabric retained its **lanuginous** surface.

  a. ☐ shiny

  b. ☐ colored

  c. ☐ metallic

  d. ☐ downy

  e. ☐ attractive

10. Will he ever cease favoring us with his **jeremiads?**

  a. ☐ optimistic predictions

  b. ☐ unreasoned criticisms

  c. ☐ easy explanations

  d. ☐ long mournful laments

  e. ☐ prophetic statements

■ *ZINGERS*

A. **dottle:**

  a. ☐ small dowry intended for one's youngest daughter

  b. ☐ unburned tobacco left in a pipe

  c. ☐ indication of senility

  d. ☐ impediment to progress

  e. ☐ incentive to increase effort

B. **marasmus:**

a. ☐ dyed silken fabric

b. ☐ artificial coloring for fruit

c. ☐ progressive emaciation

d. ☐ inability to achieve binocular vision

e. ☐ residue of glacial action

Test
<u>SEVEN</u>

1. Try as the boy would, he could not keep from **retching.**

a. ☐ scratching oneself to the point of drawing blood

b. ☐ yielding to thoughts of doing harm to others

c. ☐ straining the throat as if in vomiting

d. ☐ withdrawing into oneself

e. ☐ abandoning all hope for the future

2. It soon became obvious we were dealing with a person who could be described most charitably as **quixotic.**

a. ☐ somewhat adventurous

b. ☐ impractically idealistic

c. ☐ almost irrepressible

d. ☐ somewhat excitable

e. ☐ mildly enthusiastic

3. Everyone agreed he would never do as a **raconteur** even though he thought of himself as outstanding in that role.

a. ☐ financial analyst

b. ☐ intelligence operative

c. ☐ stock market expert

d. □   labor mediator

e. □   teller of anecdotes

4. All Alice could think of throughout the day was what she could possibly talk about with the distinguished men and women she surely would meet at the **soiree.**

   a. □   séance

   b. □   social evening

   c. □   dinner party

   d. □   lecture

   e. □   fashionable resort

5. Once the **tambour** was put aside, everyone present looked ahead to the remainder of the evening's program with great anticipation.

   a. □   drum

   b. □   string instrument

   c. □   medieval horn

   d. □   baton

   e. □   lute

6. They could only marvel at the unself-conscious way in which Mark offered one **sanctimonious** statement after another.

   a. □   thoroughly vindictive

   b. □   hypocritically courteous

   c. □   making a show of righteousness

   d. □   thoughtfully conceived

   e. □   pretending to exhibit great knowledge

7. **Oviparous** animals are useful to mankind.

   a. □   given to bearing more than a single offspring at one time

   b. □   producing eggs that are fertilized within the body of the mother

21

c. ☐ producing eggs that are fertilized after they leave the body of the mother

d. ☐ producing eggs that develop and hatch outside the mother's body

e. ☐ producing eggs that require no further attention by the mother

8. Matisse, among his many other artistic accomplishments, conceived and executed beautiful designs for **sacerdotal** robes.

a. ☐ sacred

b. ☐ priestly

c. ☐ patrician

d. ☐ silken

e. ☐ judicial

9. Many valuable texts have been recovered from **palimpsests** that long have been overlooked in classical libraries.

a. ☐ writing surfaces on which original writing has been erased and something else written

b. ☐ parchment scrolls used for writing in the Middle Ages

c. ☐ papyrus scrolls of the ancient Egyptians

d. ☐ clay tablets used by the Phoenicians

e. ☐ ancient Greek manuscripts

10. They were looked upon as nothing more than **lubricious** drawings of an immature artist.

a. ☐ unsatisfactory

b. ☐ ill-conceived

c. ☐ incompletely executed

d. ☐ ill-intentioned

e. ☐ lewd

■ *ZINGERS*

A. **metonymy:**

a. ☐ use of words whose sounds represent the intended meanings

b. ☐ substitution of the name of an attribute for the name of the thing meant

c. ☐ change in relative order between sounds or letters in a word

d. ☐ use of an exaggerated statement not meant to be taken literally

e. ☐ application of a name or descriptive term to something to which it is not literally applicable

B. **abomasum:**

a. ☐ member of a secret fraternal order

b. ☐ responsibility of a plantation overseer

c. ☐ distance between waterline and deck of a ship

d. ☐ true digestive stomach of a ruminant

e. ☐ expression of extreme disgust and loathing

Test
EIGHT

1. Charlatans who once promoted the sale of **elixirs** to gullible 19th-century men and women have their modern counterparts in the TV pitchmen who extol a variety of vitamins, painkillers, and deodorants.

a. ☐ remedies effective in curing all ills

b. ☐ salves encouraging the growth of hair

c. ☐ remedies for the common cold

d. ☐ aromatic headache powders

e. ☐ cures for upset stomachs

2. Early in Smith's career, newspaper columnists saw him as a **demagogue,** and he was never able to overcome that perception.

a. ☐ leader who stops at nothing to force his opinions on others

b. ☐ unscrupulous politician who seeks power by underhanded means

c. ☐ advocate of higher taxes without benefit to the people who elect him

d. ☐ leader who seeks power by appealing to popular prejudices

e. ☐ leader who promotes causes that advance the interests of his supporters

3. Modern audiences fail to grasp the **connotations** of much of the language used in Restoration comedy.

a. ☐ satiric intentions

b. ☐ contemporary references

c. ☐ implied meanings

d. ☐ political allusions

e. ☐ double meanings

4. **Zealous** efforts of her principal supporters in promoting her candidacy proved no match for the rational arguments advanced by the opposition.

a. ☐ persistently ferocious

b. ☐ ardently diligent

c. ☐ openly partisan

d. ☐ annoyingly disputatious

e. ☐ carefully planned

5. As we predicted, Kathleen found the Florida climate **enervating.**

    a. ☐ greatly invigorating

    b. ☐ mildly invigorating

    c. ☐ helpful for the nerves

    d. ☐ generally mild

    e. ☐ physically weakening

6. The physician said there was no pressing reason to remove the **wen.**

    a. ☐ stomach ulcer in early stage of growth

    b. ☐ cyst growing on the skin

    c. ☐ polyp growing on mucous membrane

    d. ☐ encrustation on the scalp

    e. ☐ wart

7. When the boys' choir appeared, resplendent in freshly laundered **surplices,** all parents present beamed in anticipation of the music they were about to hear.

    a. ☐ full-length white choral robes

    b. ☐ white cassocks and caps

    c. ☐ sleeveless white linen vestments usually reaching to the hips

    d. ☐ loose white outer vestments usually reaching to the knees

    e. ☐ white cloaklike vestments usually reaching to the floor

8. Ron's friends were astonished to find how soon after marriage he became **uxorious.**

    a. ☐ properly attentive

    b. ☐ loving and caring

    c. ☐ well-intentioned and home-loving

d. ☐ inconsiderate

e. ☐ overly submissive

9. The new judge's **tendentious** public statements inevitably brought her behavior to the attention of judicial review boards.

a. ☐ highly subjective

b. ☐ intended to attract publicity

c. ☐ intended to support a particular cause

d. ☐ intended to enhance progress in a career

e. ☐ intemperate and ill-considered

10. The committee's **sedulous** pursuit of all the facts in the matter brought favorable comment in the press.

a. ☐ persevering and diligent

b. ☐ rapid and thorough

c. ☐ objective and complete

d. ☐ intelligent and skillful

e. ☐ considerate and insightful

■ *ZINGERS*

A. **treillage:**

a. ☐ pity

b. ☐ trellis

c. ☐ troika

d. ☐ dotage

e. ☐ drayage

B. **hebetude:**

a. ☐ despondency

b. ☐ covetousness

c. ☐ decay

d. ☐ disrepair

e. ☐ lethargy

Test
NINE

1. Investigators concluded that someone in the mail room had been **filching** postage stamps.

   a. ☐ collecting

   b. ☐ canceling

   c. ☐ stealing

   d. ☐ borrowing

   e. ☐ selling

2. By the time the merger was concluded, the firm had earned a reputation for **callous** treatment of its employees.

   a. ☐ unsympathetic

   b. ☐ discriminatory

   c. ☐ objective

   d. ☐ cautious

   e. ☐ humane

3. All members of the caucus agreed it would make good sense to **espouse** the radical position.

   a. ☐ ignore

   b. ☐ oppose

   c. ☐ investigate

   d. ☐ overrule

   e. ☐ support

27

4. Much to our surprise, the minority leader charged out of the hall in a **dudgeon.**

   a. ☐   state of deep despair

   b. ☐   state of elation

   c. ☐   state of indignation

   d. ☐   state of revulsion

   e. ☐   great hurry

5. Customs officials found evidence of large-scale traffic in **amphorae** during the busy tourist season.

   a. ☐   prescription drugs

   b. ☐   stimulants of the central nervous system

   c. ☐   rare Turkish water pipes

   d. ☐   ancient Greek or Roman two-handled vases

   e. ☐   aromatic smoking tobaccos

6. Eventually, the reporter's **apocryphal** account of the scandal in government gained wide acceptance.

   a. ☐   factual

   b. ☐   exaggerated

   c. ☐   inaccurate

   d. ☐   accurate

   e. ☐   invented

7. In that decade **clerestories** almost became architectural clichés.

   a. ☐   outside walls of rooms rising above adjoining roofs and containing high windows

   b. ☐   cathedral ceilings decorated with mosaics

   c. ☐   living rooms containing picture windows

   d. ☐   living rooms sunk below the levels of adjoining rooms

   e. ☐   bathtubs sunk below floor level

8. Despite the administration of **humectants,** her patient's health continued to decline.

   a. ☐   substances that clear the nasal passages

   b. ☐   substances that promote retention of moisture

   c. ☐   substances that control spitting and coughing

   d. ☐   substances that increase muscle tone

   e. ☐   substances that reduce blood pressure

9. After many years of study, the group began to comprehend the meaning of **dharma.**

   a. ☐   Buddhist ethical doctrine

   b. ☐   Buddhist concept of self-reliance

   c. ☐   Buddhist advocacy of charity

   d. ☐   Buddhist moral law

   e. ☐   Buddhist force determining destiny

10. Would they have behaved differently if they had known from the start their ideal society was an **ignis fatuus?**

   a. ☐   fait accompli

   b. ☐   delusive hope

   c. ☐   incendiary doctrine

   d. ☐   illogical conception

   e. ☐   probable failure

■   *ZINGERS*

A. **ennead:**

   a. ☐   cause for despair

   b. ☐   novel proposal

   c. ☐   group of nine

   d. ☐   sea nymph

   e. ☐   object of admiration

B. **operose:**

a. ☐ laborious
b. ☐ extravagant
c. ☐ outrageous
d. ☐ deceitful
e. ☐ vain

Test
TEN

1. Two of the bigger boys are said to have **pummeled** the smallest boy in the class while the other students watched.

a. ☐ tormented
b. ☐ struck repeatedly
c. ☐ teased mercilessly
d. ☐ insulted
e. ☐ provoked cruelly

2. The **ignominious** outcome was predictable by anyone with sense who had taken all relevant factors into account.

a. ☐ unforeseen
b. ☐ unspeakable
c. ☐ humiliating
d. ☐ inevitable
e. ☐ obvious

3. Who could resist a second helping of the delicious **ragout?**

a. ☐ thick meat soup
b. ☐ rich dessert

c. □ side dish of pickled vegetables

d. □ puree of cooked vegetables

e. □ stew of vegetables and meat

4. **Agoraphobia** is far from uncommon today.

a. □ abnormal fear of being at great heights

b. □ abnormal fear of crossing open spaces

c. □ abnormal fear of being alone in darkness

d. □ abnormal fear of meeting foreigners

e. □ abnormal fear of flying

5. The president's advisers seem oblivious to the danger of **internecine** warfare.

a. □ mutually destructive

b. □ protracted

c. □ seemingly endless

d. □ mindless

e. □ undertaken to settle long-standing disputes

6. What turned out be a **draconian** policy was undertaken with the best of intentions.

a. □ impossible to reverse

b. □ poorly carried out

c. □ ineptly prepared

d. □ very harsh

e. □ completely unacceptable

7. Who is brave enough to **flout** regulations that are obviously harmful to the company's goals?

a. □ disobey openly

b. □ point out

c. □ discuss publicly

    d. ☐   reveal to others

    e. ☐   find fault with

8. The program concluded with yet another **orotund** statement from the chairman of the board.

    a. ☐   carefully worded

    b. ☐   wordy

    c. ☐   pretentious

    d. ☐   anecdotal

    e. ☐   concise and well-reasoned

9. No one yet knows who will next serve as **locum tenens**.

    a. ☐   person second in command

    b. ☐   lieutenant

    c. ☐   presiding officer

    d. ☐   principal advocate

    e. ☐   deputy

10. Few of us can see ourselves living the life of an **eremite**.

    a. ☐   religious dissenter

    b. ☐   religious recluse

    c. ☐   lonely leader

    d. ☐   saint

    e. ☐   devoutly religious person

■ *ZINGERS*

A. **henotheism:** belief in

    a. ☐   a benevolent god

    b. ☐   nature as the true deity

    c. ☐   a wrathful god

d. ☐ one god without asserting there is only one god

e. ☐ one god as foremost among all the gods

B. **scilicet:**

a. ☐ as written

b. ☐ as spoken

c. ☐ namely

d. ☐ and the opposite

e. ☐ and the following

Test
<u>ELEVEN</u>

1. Last season the **paucity** of readily available raw materials caused us to modify our production plan.

a. ☐ oversupply

b. ☐ high quality

c. ☐ unavailability

d. ☐ inadequate supply

e. ☐ poor quality

2. The last thing we need is another **ketch.**

a. ☐ soil-building plant

b. ☐ annoying person

c. ☐ type of sailboat

d. ☐ greenhouse

e. ☐ memory jogger

3. The presentation began with a **cogent** analysis of the situation.

    a. ☐ convincing

    b. ☐ thoughtful

    c. ☐ simplified

    d. ☐ quick but thorough

    e. ☐ clever

4. Once you have seen a **phalarope,** you never will forget it.

    a. ☐ marsupial mammal

    b. ☐ musical instrument resembling an organ

    c. ☐ passion play

    d. ☐ small shorebird

    e. ☐ Egyptian representation of a god

5. One feature of the journal is its up-to-date **necrology.**

    a. ☐ statistical table of fatal diseases

    b. ☐ list of those who have died

    c. ☐ continuing study of causes of death

    d. ☐ bibliography on the subject of death

    e. ☐ statistical prediction of death rates

6. Advocates of **homeopathy** may encounter resistance among traditional physicians.

    a. ☐ medical treatment employing substances readily available in the home

    b. ☐ medical treatment employing substances occurring naturally

    c. ☐ medical treatment based on Eastern practices

    d. ☐ medical teatment employing all techniques available except surgery

    e. ☐ medical treatment employing small doses of drugs that produce symptoms of disease

7. Once again his subject was an **odalisque,** but this time he worked in oils rather than crayon.

   a. ☐　female slave in a harem

   b. ☐　woman of great beauty

   c. ☐　peasant woman

   d. ☐　factory girl

   e. ☐　religious figure

8. In the opinion of most of those present, the **palanquin** had seen better days.

   a. ☐　settee

   b. ☐　saddle horse

   c. ☐　litter

   d. ☐　boat

   e. ☐　wall decoration

9. Bank examiners determined that most of our loans were not **fungible.**

   a. ☐　collectible

   b. ☐　interchangeable

   c. ☐　long-term

   d. ☐　documented

   e. ☐　backed up by collateral

10. Have you ever known anyone who lived by a set of truly **irrefragable** principles?

   a. ☐　unalterable

   b. ☐　unimpeachable

   c. ☐　inimitable

   d. ☐　unfounded

   e. ☐　imperfect

■ *ZINGERS*

A. **perron:**

a. ☐   stone wall intended only as decoration

b. ☐   outdoor stairway to a building entrance

c. ☐   mildly fermented drink made of pear juice

d. ☐   stone of gem quality

e. ☐   single unit of an ordered set of objects

B. **reboant:**

a. ☐   increasing

b. ☐   rebuking

c. ☐   reviving

d. ☐   incremental

e. ☐   resounding

Test
TWELVE

1. In that climate no freeze can be called **untimely.**

a. ☐   unseasonable

b. ☐   late

c. ☐   welcome

d. ☐   unwelcome

e. ☐   anticipated

2. They **writhed** in pain during the entire time we were with them.

a. ☐   cried out

b. ☐   twisted about

c. ☐   silently suffered

d. ☐ wrung their hands

e. ☐ prayed for relief

3. We studied the **vernacular** as well as we could in the months available to us.

    a. ☐ gutter speech

    b. ☐ mixture of two or more languages

    c. ☐ language of a particular group

    d. ☐ slang of a particular group

    e. ☐ language of uneducated people

4. An **unmitigated** awkwardness characterizes most people of our age.

    a. ☐ unsurpassed

    b. ☐ unqualified

    c. ☐ unnatural

    d. ☐ unimaginable

    e. ☐ unseemly

5. It was the number of **wadis** found in the region that interested scientists.

    a. ☐ slight elevations in desert terrain

    b. ☐ wandering tribes able to sustain themselves in desert environments

    c. ☐ desert animals

    d. ☐ stream beds dry except during rainy seasons

    e. ☐ oases capable of supplying water throughout the year

6. The variety of **viviparous** animals present in that environment astonished most observers.

    a. ☐ fur-bearing

    b. ☐ aquatic

   c. ☐ warm-blooded

   d. ☐ able to withstand extremes in climate

   e. ☐ producing living offspring

7. In the area in which they found mineral springs, **tufa** predominated.

   a. ☐ spongy terrain

   b. ☐ marshland

   c. ☐ porous rock

   d. ☐ reeds and grasses

   e. ☐ sandy soil

8. The justice's reputation was based primarily on her unfailing, **rhadamanthine** pronouncements.

   a. ☐ sternly just

   b. ☐ far-reaching

   c. ☐ crystal clear

   d. ☐ carefully considered

   e. ☐ objective

9. **Mycology** does not seem to attract many of our graduate students.

   a. ☐ study of fungi

   b. ☐ study of muscles

   c. ☐ study of bone marrow

   d. ☐ study of microscopic organisms

   e. ☐ study of nerve fibers

10. Our bookkeeping does not take **ullage** into account.

   a. ☐ refusal of a shipment of goods

   b. ☐ amount by which a cask is less than full

   c. ☐ cost of shipment of merchandise to final destination

d. ☐ discount for purchase of merchandise in large quantities

e. ☐ professional discount for goods ordered

■ *ZINGERS*

A. **haruspex:**

a. ☐ horseman

b. ☐ vivisectionist

c. ☐ interrogator

d. ☐ soothsayer

e. ☐ phlebotomist

B. **viduity:**

a. ☐ impossibility

b. ☐ futility

c. ☐ widowhood

d. ☐ vacuity

e. ☐ decay

Test
THIRTEEN

1. Who would have expected a person so young to deliver a **eulogy** so moving?

a. ☐ keynote speech

b. ☐ introductory statement

c. ☐ commencement speech

d. ☐ valedictory

e. ☐ funeral oration

2. Our reviews run the **gamut** from faint praise to passionate condemnation.

    a. ☐   cross fire

    b. ☐   entire range

    c. ☐   ordeal

    d. ☐   critical response

    e. ☐   anticipated reaction

3. I parted company with my friends because they ultimately proved **intransigent.**

    a. ☐   insensitive

    b. ☐   unwilling to improve

    c. ☐   incapable of sharing responsibility

    d. ☐   uncompromising

    e. ☐   lacking in ambition

4. A **piebald** horse is certainly not my first choice.

    a. ☐   blind in one eye

    b. ☐   poorly trained

    c. ☐   of two different colors

    d. ☐   nearly hairless

    e. ☐   of slow pace

5. It seemed likely the two factions would never **coalesce.**

    a. ☐   unite for a common purpose

    b. ☐   abandon a common goal

    c. ☐   recognize common danger

    d. ☐   settle disputes

    e. ☐   compromise on a course of action

6. Who decided to **immolate** the offering?

   a. ☐ reduce

   b. ☐ retain

   c. ☐ destroy

   d. ☐ remove

   e. ☐ increase

7. The veteran scout was never seen without his **firkin.**

   a. ☐ leather vest

   b. ☐ small cask

   c. ☐ horse

   d. ☐ small-caliber weapon

   e. ☐ leather belt

8. Whenever the sisters visited one another, they inevitably would retell stories of their **halcyon** days.

   a. ☐ happy

   b. ☐ youthful

   c. ☐ innocent

   d. ☐ childhood

   e. ☐ early

9. Economic hardship is recognized as the root cause of the black **diaspora.**

   a. ☐ struggle for political recognition

   b. ☐ resurgent pride

   c. ☐ turning inward for support

   d. ☐ rejection of imposed standards of conduct

   e. ☐ dispersion of a group of people

10. David was essentially a **Manichean** in a society of conventional thinkers.

   a. ☐ one who believes the universe is ruled by opposing forces of good and evil

   b. ☐ one who believes the struggle between good and evil will be won by goodness

   c. ☐ one who rejects the belief that evil forces exist in the universe

   d. ☐ one who believes people can shape their own destinies

   e. ☐ one who rejects the doctrine of salvation through good works

■   *ZINGERS*

A. **pilgarlic:**

   a. ☐ natural-food advocate

   b. ☐ bald-headed man

   c. ☐ seasoning for otherwise bland food

   d. ☐ hapless gardener

   e. ☐ greengrocer

B. **fuscous:**

   a. ☐ overly pompous

   b. ☐ deliberately annoying

   c. ☐ given to banality

   d. ☐ somber

   e. ☐ evil

Test
FOURTEEN

1. My neighbor's dog is known throughout the area for its **bellicosity.**

   a. ☐ striking beauty

   b. ☐ inclination to fight

   c. ☐ friendliness

   d. ☐ ability to frighten strangers

   e. ☐ fierce appearance

2. Our business showed an **infinitesimal** profit last year.

   a. ☐ record-breaking

   b. ☐ excellent

   c. ☐ relatively poor

   d. ☐ immeasurably small

   e. ☐ extraordinary

3. The ultimate goal of the popular movement is political **hegemony.**

   a. ☐ equality

   b. ☐ independence

   c. ☐ suffrage

   d. ☐ separation

   e. ☐ predominance

4. Everyone assembled in the **refectory** early that morning.

   a. ☐ dining room

   b. ☐ chief administrative office

   c. ☐ assembly hall

d. ☐   mirrored salon

e. ☐   common room

5. My **captious** daughter was the only one in the family who expressed no serious doubt.

a. ☐   inclined to seek a peaceful solution

b. ☐   inclined to show superior knowledge

c. ☐   inclined to be openly hostile

d. ☐   inclined to display pessimism

e. ☐   inclined to raise objections

6. Who does not marvel at her ability to construct lengthy **palindromes?**

a. ☐   apt metaphors

b. ☐   words or sentences reading the same backward and forward

c. ☐   evocative passages committed to memory

d. ☐   glittering examples of literary parody

e. ☐   orations intended to evoke sympathy for one's cause by citing examples of historic injustice

7. The functioning of the **nictitating** membrane is well understood by physiologists.

a. ☐   lubricating

b. ☐   protective

c. ☐   winking

d. ☐   tearing

e. ☐   supporting

8. For the first time, the young physician had to deal with a widespread incidence of **emesis.**

   a. ☐   skin ulcers

   b. ☐   protracted high fever

   c. ☐   fungus infection

   d. ☐   vomiting

   e. ☐   dysentery

9. Elizabeth's **preternatural** intelligence became immediately apparent to all members of the board.

   a. ☐   extraordinary

   b. ☐   admirable

   c. ☐   adequate

   d. ☐   less than adequate

   e. ☐   more than adequate

10. To the very end, despite our repeated requests, she would not discuss the secret of her once-acclaimed **penuche.**

   a. ☐   verve

   b. ☐   hidden wealth

   c. ☐   fudge

   d. ☐   ability to attract admirers

   e. ☐   great love

■ *ZINGERS*

A. **favonian:** of the

   a. ☐   east wind

   b. ☐   west wind

   c. ☐   north wind

   d. ☐   south wind

   e. ☐   primordial wind

B. **rhonchus:**

a. ☐   sound perceived while holding an empty conch to the ear

b. ☐   sound signaling the imminence of death

c. ☐   ringing sound perceived as a result of infection in the inner ear

d. ☐   rattling sound heard in clogged bronchial tubes

e. ☐   piercing sound preceding some types of coronary seizures

Test
FIFTEEN

1. His **effeminacy** was taken for granted by the majority of his students.

a. ☐   unmanliness

b. ☐   concern for women's causes

c. ☐   concern for political rights

d. ☐   harsh treatment of women

e. ☐   unrestrained enthusiasm

2. **Chauvinist** movements characterized that period in world history.

a. ☐   favoring self-government

b. ☐   missionary

c. ☐   excessively patriotic

d. ☐   imperialist

e. ☐   cooperative

3. How an **obsequious** person retains any self-respect is beyond me.

   a. ☐ overly ambitious
   b. ☐ showing disdain for others
   c. ☐ completely self-centered
   d. ☐ interested only in power
   e. ☐ servile

4. His **gaffes** were memorable but did nothing to advance his candidacy.

   a. ☐ clever statements
   b. ☐ unselfish acts
   c. ☐ personal appearances
   d. ☐ indiscreet remarks
   e. ☐ political blunders

5. I refuse to **remonstrate** with such a person.

   a. ☐ confront vigorously
   b. ☐ plead in protest
   c. ☐ appear publicly
   d. ☐ engage in discussion
   e. ☐ debate important issues

6. What we need is a serviceable **screed.**

   a. ☐ board used for leveling concrete
   b. ☐ transparent theatrical curtain
   c. ☐ large spirit level
   d. ☐ tool used for crimping electrical wire
   e. ☐ versatile screwdriver

7. The characteristic **panache** he once displayed was no longer in evidence.

a. ☐   lack of confidence

b. ☐   concern for the welfare of others

c. ☐   confident stylish manner

d. ☐   unawareness of the feelings of others

e. ☐   absorption in self

8. Nothing we tried could dispel the effects of the **miasma** we encountered.

a. ☐   widespread gloom

b. ☐   absolute depravity

c. ☐   intellectual dishonesty

d. ☐   prevailing commercial dishonesty

e. ☐   dangerous atmosphere

9. Our group's **imprimatur** was eagerly sought as a means of realizing the full commercial potential of the work.

a. ☐   skill in printing

b. ☐   talent for publicity

c. ☐   sanction

d. ☐   financial support

e. ☐   political power

10. Their principal works of **hagiography** were not translated until this century.

a. ☐   explanation of mystical practices

b. ☐   biography of saints

c. ☐   definition of classical conceptions of philosophy

d. ☐   explanation of primitive practices

e. ☐   description of ancient societies

■ *ZINGERS*

A. **wharfinger:**

a. ☐   operator of a wharf

b. ☐   arthritic joint

c. ☐   identifying mark or characteristic

d. ☐   destructive fungus

e. ☐   premonition

B. **viaticum:**

a. ☐   brief vacation

b. ☐   wayside shrine

c. ☐   money for a journey

d. ☐   personal prayer book

e. ☐   choice among permanent assignments

Test
SIXTEEN

1. Holders of credit cards must beware of waking up one morning and finding themselves in a financial **quagmire.**

a. ☐   nightmare

b. ☐   state of bankruptcy

c. ☐   very difficult situation

d. ☐   condition in which debts grow uncontrollably

e. ☐   condition in which further purchases are impossible

2. I have always been wary of people who pay **effusive** compliments.

   a. ☐   unduly demonstrative

   b. ☐   begrudgingly given

   c. ☐   obviously unearned

   d. ☐   left-handed

   e. ☐   ill-considered

3. Weariness set in after two hours, yet the conversation could still have been described as **scintillating.**

   a. ☐   sparkling

   b. ☐   flowing freely

   c. ☐   annoying

   d. ☐   resulting in hurt feelings

   e. ☐   shedding valuable light

4. Jane's instructor said her **hyperbole** was unacceptable.

   a. ☐   long-winded excuse

   b. ☐   extravagant statement not meant to be taken literally

   c. ☐   geometric proof

   d. ☐   illogical conclusion based on incomplete investigation

   e. ☐   outburst of irrational behavior

5. When towns **burgeon,** we must question whether the advantages outweigh the disadvantages.

   a. ☐   lose original character

   b. ☐   increase economic vitality

   c. ☐   begin to grow rapidly

   d. ☐   build indiscriminately

   e. ☐   exclude most types of industry

6. The defense attorney adopted **obfuscation** as her only hope for dismissal of the charges.

a. ☐ repeated delaying tactics

b. ☐ emotional argumentation

c. ☐ appeals to individual conscience

d. ☐ obscuration

e. ☐ attacks on the credibility of witnesses

7. His discussion of the **krummholz** interested only those who had known in advance that the lecturer had chosen that topic.

a. ☐ a type of medieval wind instrument

b. ☐ a type of leguminous vine

c. ☐ a type of fur

d. ☐ a type of burial mound

e. ☐ a type of stunted forest

8. The last thing the couple needed was another **cachepot.**

a. ☐ kitchen cabinet

b. ☐ ornamental container concealing a flowerpot

c. ☐ teapot

d. ☐ scented handkerchief

e. ☐ room deodorizer

9. The **girasol** went unnoticed by most of the fashionable people at the party.

a. ☐ theatrical entrance

b. ☐ unconventional departure

c. ☐ type of opal

d. ☐ disreputable behavior

e. ☐ unrestrained laughter

10. In the absence of hard evidence, the statement clearly was an **illation.**

a. ☐ inferred conclusion
b. ☐ unsupported guess
c. ☐ shaky hypothesis
d. ☐ unwarranted inference
e. ☐ generalization awaiting precise definition

■ *ZINGERS*

A. **altricial:** of birds that

a. ☐ build rudimentary nests
b. ☐ lay fewer than three eggs
c. ☐ die shortly after hatching
d. ☐ must be fed by parents after hatching
e. ☐ have not yet been fledged

B. **lapsus calami:**

a. ☐ slip of the pen
b. ☐ slip of the memory
c. ☐ slip of the tongue
d. ☐ error in judgment
e. ☐ social blunder

Test
SEVENTEEN

1. We all suspected she would prove **adamant** in refusing to grant interviews.

    a. ☐   correct in judgment

    b. ☐   quite firm

    c. ☐   sincere

    d. ☐   totally wrong

    e. ☐   offensive in manner

2. The **tether** we bought broke after just a few days' use.

    a. ☐   leather strip used as a lash or fastening

    b. ☐   metal or leather support for a horseback rider's feet

    c. ☐   highest bar of a fence used for enclosing young horses

    d. ☐   rope or chain used to fasten a grazing animal

    e. ☐   metal bar forming the mouthpiece of a bridle

3. The decision to resort to **scrip** was taken in order to prevent further problems.

    a. ☐   paper currency for use in emergencies

    b. ☐   written text for a performance

    c. ☐   careful budgeting of household expenses

    d. ☐   recycled household material

    e. ☐   household remedies used in place of prescription drugs

4. I found his **rejoinders** refreshing despite the fact that they sometimes hurt.

    a. ☐   witty remarks

    b. ☐   observations

    c. ☐   insights

d. ☐   questions

e. ☐   replies

5. The last thing we expected was a series of completely **ingenuous** responses to our questions.

a. ☐   frank

b. ☐   ambiguous

c. ☐   deceptive

d. ☐   clever

e. ☐   hostile

6. A history of ethical behavior in private and public life is a **desideratum** in candidates for high office.

a. ☐   something lacking that is seldom obtained

b. ☐   something lacking that is undesirable

c. ☐   something lacking that is essential to obtain

d. ☐   something lacking that is difficult to obtain

e. ☐   something lacking that is impossible to obtain

7. The auctioneer represented the piece as an excellent example of **faience.**

a. ☐   primitive representation of a deity

b. ☐   Etruscan or Roman statuary

c. ☐   glazed earthenware or porcelain

d. ☐   wall hanging or painting

e. ☐   Russian iconography

8. Attorneys in the United States seldom face a charge of **barratry.**

a. ☐   inappropriate behavior in a courtroom

b. ☐   improper contact with an officer of the court

c. ☐   failure to represent a client adequately

d. ☐ excessive delay in responding to a legal writ

e. ☐ annoying incitement to litigation

9. Social workers at the shelter assured us that the child's tantrums were **adventitious.**

a. ☐ diminishing in number

b. ☐ occurring sporadically

c. ☐ diminishing in severity

d. ☐ expected

e. ☐ bound to disappear

10. Frequency of **micturition** appeared to be well within normal limits.

a. ☐ sexual contact

b. ☐ irregular heartbeat

c. ☐ urination

d. ☐ absence from work

e. ☐ shallow breathing

■ *ZINGERS*

A. **thimblerig:**

a. ☐ elaborate contraption

b. ☐ shell game

c. ☐ jury rig

d. ☐ safety device used in sewing

e. ☐ temporary apparatus

B. **stridulate:**

a. ☐ persist in complaining

b. ☐ lengthen stride in walking or running

c. ☐   howl

d. ☐   make a shrill jarring sound

e. ☐   seek to attract attention

Test
<u>EIGHTEEN</u>

1. Anne's never-failing **dexterity** astounded us once again.

a. ☐   self-righteousness

b. ☐   inappropriate response

c. ☐   narrow-mindedness

d. ☐   skill in handling things

e. ☐   correctness in social behavior

2. **Guano** still has great commercial value in some parts of the world.

a. ☐   dung of seabirds

b. ☐   type of tropical fruit

c. ☐   type of freshwater fish

d. ☐   residue of the brewing process

e. ☐   pulp of grapes used in making wine

3. By then, we all thought she was resigned to her husband's habitual **carping.**

a. ☐   harsh criticism

b. ☐   petty faultfinding

c. ☐   rejection of criticism

d. ☐   uncontrolled spending

e. ☐   scrimping

4. **Pejorative** comments are the rule when my college friends get together.

a. ☐ disparaging
b. ☐ helpful
c. ☐ implying suspicion of motives
d. ☐ expressing complete trust
e. ☐ satirical

5. How many times did Tom's father say, "You are the **bane** of my life"?

a. ☐ single most important factor
b. ☐ principal financial drain
c. ☐ cause of trouble
d. ☐ least important factor
e. ☐ center of interest

6. At the start of his career, most critics dismissed him as a **yahoo.**

a. ☐ sports fanatic
b. ☐ uncouth person
c. ☐ disagreeable person
d. ☐ person of narrow interests
e. ☐ outcast

7. Close examination revealed that it was surely a **pismire.**

a. ☐ decomposed animal
b. ☐ irrigating ditch
c. ☐ water gun
d. ☐ ant
e. ☐ marsh

8. For a while, at least, his **jejune** behavior made him the center of attention.

 a. ☐ precocious

 b. ☐ childish

 c. ☐ astonishing

 d. ☐ unconventional

 e. ☐ impossible

9. During the student strike there were **hebdomadal** faculty meetings.

 a. ☐ hourly

 b. ☐ daily

 c. ☐ nightly

 d. ☐ semiweekly

 e. ☐ weekly

10. Edith's associates looked upon her as their **paladin.**

 a. ☐ champion of a cause

 b. ☐ benevolent dictator

 c. ☐ principal adversary

 d. ☐ leading strategist

 e. ☐ intellectual leader

■ ZINGERS

A. **vicennial:** lasting or occurring every

 a. ☐ five years

 b. ☐ fifteen years

 c. ☐ twenty years

 d. ☐ twenty-five years

 e. ☐ fifty years

B. **gongoristic:**

a. ☐ satiric
b. ☐ naturalistic
c. ☐ euphuistic
d. ☐ parodic
e. ☐ romantic

Test
NINETEEN

1. His **ribald** jokes quickly made their way through the company.

a. ☐ lacking humor
b. ☐ coarsely humorous
c. ☐ obvious
d. ☐ suggestive of racism
e. ☐ stale

2. Edwin's **pretentious** manner actually helped his career.

a. ☐ offensive
b. ☐ unrealistic
c. ☐ showy
d. ☐ dishonest
e. ☐ lacking sincerity

3. In adolescence **ornithology** was her principal interest.

a. ☐ study of word origins
b. ☐ study of human anatomy
c. ☐ study of myths and legends

    d. ☐   study of reptiles

    e. ☐   study of birds

4. Was Barbara really willing to make the effort needed for intellectual survival in the **welter** of academic life on that campus?

    a. ☐   slow decline

    b. ☐   state of turmoil

    c. ☐   challenging environment

    d. ☐   undemanding environment

    e. ☐   unrestricted freedom

5. The New England peddler of times past lives on today as a **vulpine** dealer in antiques.

    a. ☐   crafty

    b. ☐   itinerant

    c. ☐   talkative

    d. ☐   small-scale

    e. ☐   common in manner

6. The effects of a **tsunami** soon become apparent.

    a. ☐   first tropical storm of a season

    b. ☐   storm originating over Japan

    c. ☐   major earthquake followed by strong aftershocks

    d. ☐   series of huge sea waves

    e. ☐   unpredictable volcanic eruption

7. Of a long and tranquil summer evening, Fred was known to **maunder.**

    a. ☐   wander in a leisurely way

    b. ☐   dwell on small matters

    c. ☐   sit quietly for long periods

d. ☐   seek solitude

e. ☐   talk in a rambling way

8. Until modern times, the **pyknic** body type was the most prevalent in that climate.

a. ☐   of short stature

b. ☐   having thick neck, short limbs, broad abdomen

c. ☐   of light build, with narrow chest and long limbs

d. ☐   lightly muscled and short-legged

e. ☐   heavily muscled and long-legged

9. We must not ignore **ontogeny** in our discussion of evolution.

a. ☐   creation of individual differences

b. ☐   process by which one individual becomes dominant over others

c. ☐   development of an individual organism

d. ☐   role of an individual organism in establishing group characteristics

e. ☐   process by which a species is created

10. Much of the debate was no more than **logomachy.**

a. ☐   dispute over words

b. ☐   scholarly hairsplitting

c. ☐   unsupported assertion

d. ☐   general lack of understanding

e. ☐   verbal abuse

■   *ZINGERS*

A. **yashmak:**

a. ☐   shroud

b. ☐   veil

c. ☐   hair net

d. ☐   head covering

e. ☐   long gown

B. **pelisse:**

a. ☐   fur collar

b. ☐   royal court costume

c. ☐   ermine outer jacket

d. ☐   fur-lined cloak

e. ☐   animal skin

Test
<u>TWENTY</u>

1. Nothing you say will **besmirch** their reputations.

a. ☐   help

b. ☐   affect

c. ☐   soil

d. ☐   destroy

e. ☐   change

2. Most of us considered him nothing more than a hopeless **pedant.**

a. ☐   classical scholar and linguist

b. ☐   specialist in treating diseases of the foot

c. ☐   person who overrates book learning

d. ☐   long-distance bicyclist

e. ☐   specialist in treating diseases of children

3. We came upon a fascinating drawing of a **centaur** in the artist's notebook.

    a. ☐   Roman soldier

    b. ☐   person more than one hundred years old

    c. ☐   soldier on guard duty

    d. ☐   giant prehistoric lizard

    e. ☐   fabled half-man half-horse

4. Part of the **mandible** was also removed by the surgeon.

    a. ☐   bone of the wrist

    b. ☐   bone of the lower jaw

    c. ☐   bone of the ankle

    d. ☐   bone of the chest

    e. ☐   bone of the upper arm

5. His **querulousness** did not improve his standing in the group.

    a. ☐   habitual complaining

    b. ☐   questioning attitude

    c. ☐   inclination to pick fights

    d. ☐   cynical behavior

    e. ☐   exaggerated pettiness

6. We still recall the **ineffable** joy shown by our daughter at her first birthday party.

    a. ☐   characteristic of the young

    b. ☐   largely unrestrained

    c. ☐   unforgettable

    d. ☐   too great to be described

    e. ☐   irrepressible

7. Much of the **acropolis** still stands today.

   a. ☐   seat of government in ancient Greece

   b. ☐   temple in ancient Greece

   c. ☐   administrative building in ancient Greece

   d. ☐   market area in ancient Greece

   e. ☐   citadel of an ancient Greek city

8. During the course of Clara's definitive study of **raptorial** birds, she made numerous field trips.

   a. ☐   rare

   b. ☐   predatory

   c. ☐   tropical

   d. ☐   flightless

   e. ☐   coastal

9. One of the observers characterized the student protests as **flagitious.**

   a. ☐   utterly criminal

   b. ☐   poorly organized

   c. ☐   inciting to riot

   d. ☐   unjustifiably shrill

   e. ☐   doomed from the start

10. It is clear that even in his own time he was considered an **epigone.**

   a. ☐   skilled practitioner

   b. ☐   artist of the first rank

   c. ☐   undistinguished imitator

   d. ☐   impractical dreamer

   e. ☐   dabbler in the arts

■ *ZINGERS*

A. **sannyasi:** Hindu

a. □ faith healer

b. □ official scribe

c. □ mendicant ascetic

d. □ moral philosopher

e. □ spiritual adviser

B. **renitent:**

a. □ recalcitrant

b. □ pertaining to the kidneys

c. □ compensatory

d. □ curdling

e. □ regenerative

Test
TWENTY-ONE

1. The welcome sound of a **dulcimer** greeted us as we entered the room.

a. □ small woodwind resembling the clarinet

b. □ trumpet for ceremonial use

c. □ set of bells struck by hammers controlled from a keyboard

d. □ large violin

e. □ musical instrument with strings struck by hammers

2. Punishment for a crime so **heinous** should be considered carefully.

   a. □ very wicked

   b. □ minor in nature

   c. □ commonly encountered

   d. □ carefully planned

   e. □ commonly condoned

3. He served faithfully as **beadle** during those years.

   a. □ official parish secretary

   b. □ assistant parish treasurer

   c. □ parish officer having minor duties

   d. □ keeper of parish records

   e. □ supervisor of parish custodians

4. Charges of **calumny** were exchanged by both sides in the ensuing debate.

   a. □ unfairness

   b. □ deception

   c. □ irresponsibility

   d. □ slander

   e. □ criminal practice

5. **Fedayeen** were often seen in the bazaar during that month.

   a. □ Arab guerrillas operating against Israel

   b. □ nomadic tribesmen of the Middle East

   c. □ Arab merchants

   d. □ Muslim criers who call the faithful to prayer

   e. □ attendants at mosques in the Middle East

6. It was surely a **fortuitous** meeting.

   a. ☐ predestined

   b. ☐ carefully planned

   c. ☐ welcome

   d. ☐ highly productive

   e. ☐ happening by chance

7. We were told of a **hibernaculum** in the vicinity.

   a. ☐ winter resort

   b. ☐ winter shelter of a dormant animal

   c. ☐ sanctuary for birds in winter

   d. ☐ heated swimming pool open for use in winter

   e. ☐ winter sports area

8. The child's **lissome** body was a pleasure to observe.

   a. ☐ graceful

   b. ☐ supple

   c. ☐ athletic

   d. ☐ beautifully proportioned

   e. ☐ slender

9. Leavis and his **myrmidons** dominated the literary scene for many years.

   a. ☐ advisers

   b. ☐ admirers

   c. ☐ henchmen

   d. ☐ students

   e. ☐ close friends

10. As long as you **repine,** the situation will not improve.

   a. ☐   fret

   b. ☐   feel powerless

   c. ☐   long for love

   d. ☐   feel revulsion

   e. ☐   fail to act

   ■   *ZINGERS*

   A. **consuetude:**

   a. ☐   expression of excessive concern

   b. ☐   advanced state of decay

   c. ☐   custom having legal force

   d. ☐   justification for an action

   e. ☐   cooperative effort

   B. **inspissate:**

   a. ☐   condense

   b. ☐   liquidate

   c. ☐   evoke

   d. ☐   make useless

   e. ☐   inspire

Test
TWENTY-TWO

1. Within minutes, as my guide predicted, a beggar **accosted** me.

   a. ☐   asked for money

   b. ☐   approached and addressed

c. ☐ insulted

d. ☐ delayed

e. ☐ intimidated

2. Who among us is immune from the need to **piddle** away an afternoon now and then?

a. ☐ eat and drink to excess

b. ☐ yield to a desire to sleep

c. ☐ spend time idly

d. ☐ talk with friends

e. ☐ flirt innocently

3. Despite my best efforts, I failed in all my attempts to **beguile** them.

a. ☐ win over by threats

b. ☐ capture attention of

c. ☐ overcome disagreement with

d. ☐ dissuade through lies

e. ☐ coax by flattery

4. She was undeniably the **epitome** of fairness combined with resolve.

a. ☐ final judge

b. ☐ embodiment

c. ☐ exact opposite

d. ☐ poorest example

e. ☐ ardent advocate

5. Extent and duration of addiction were the **parameters** of greatest interest to the researchers.

a. ☐ quantifiable characteristics

b. ☐ helpful indicators

c. ☐ experimental assumptions

d. ☐ useful statistical data

e. ☐ important causative factors

6. It was apparent that the attorney **execrated** the judge's decision.

a. ☐ feared

b. ☐ deeply mistrusted

c. ☐ greatly detested

d. ☐ completely misunderstood

e. ☐ correctly anticipated

7. On our campus, **frenetic** cramming was the rule during examination week.

a. ☐ highly focused

b. ☐ single-minded

c. ☐ unproductive

d. ☐ frantic

e. ☐ obsessive

8. A **saturnine** headmaster will do little to lift student morale.

a. ☐ inclined to scheming

b. ☐ given to stern actions

c. ☐ highly judgmental

d. ☐ unfair in criticizing

e. ☐ of forbidding appearance

9. Virginia's **lambent** wit once again made itself felt.

a. ☐ quick and perceptive

b. ☐ lightly brilliant

c. ☐ undeniably insightful

d. ☐ welcome

e. ☐ spiteful

10. An **eristic** argument is not what we need now.

a. ☐ designed to establish the validity of a claim

b. ☐ skillful but dishonest

c. ☐ intended to win rather than establish truth

d. ☐ occupied with detail rather than a central issue

e. ☐ fundamentally flawed

■ *ZINGERS*

A. **exiguous:**

a. ☐ of great urgency

b. ☐ extraordinarily difficult

c. ☐ demanding

d. ☐ scanty

e. ☐ excessively critical

B. **orismology:**

a. ☐ terminology

b. ☐ time studies

c. ☐ early morning prayer

d. ☐ ornamentation

e. ☐ phenomenon usually observed at dawn

Test
TWENTY-THREE

1. From the start, the comedian's **inane** patter brought nothing but occasional laughter.

  a. ☐ lacking sense

  b. ☐ off-color

  c. ☐ somewhat funny

  d. ☐ satirical

  e. ☐ inexpertly delivered

2. Throughout Marble's career, she was considered one of the country's foremost **bibliophiles.**

  a. ☐ compilers of lists of books and articles

  b. ☐ book collectors

  c. ☐ authors of books on religion

  d. ☐ reference librarians

  e. ☐ biblical scholars

3. In photographs, his **wizened** face reminds me of my everlasting indebtedness to the man.

  a. ☐ weather-beaten

  b. ☐ showing the wisdom of experience

  c. ☐ shriveled with age

  d. ☐ kindly

  e. ☐ portrayed as gentle

4. The negotiator's **dilatory** tactics were intended to advance the union's interests.

  a. ☐ designed to embarrass

  b. ☐ designed to cause delay

  c. ☐ designed to obstruct

d. ☐   designed to confuse

e. ☐   designed to gain sympathy

5. Most of us agree that nothing can **extenuate** the president's behavior in that matter.

a. ☐   lessen seriousness of by providing a partial excuse

b. ☐   rationally explain the reasons behind

c. ☐   overcome the consequences of

d. ☐   make fully acceptable

e. ☐   surpass in quality

6. The size of your income **vitiates** your claim for special consideration.

a. ☐   immeasurably strengthens

b. ☐   amply justifies

c. ☐   has no effect on

d. ☐   fails to justify

e. ☐   makes ineffective

7. Wouldn't it be fun to have a **gecko** as a house pet?

a. ☐   type of tropical bird

b. ☐   type of tropical fish

c. ☐   type of arboreal toad

d. ☐   type of harmless lizard

e. ☐   type of freshwater fish

8. **Koans** initially confuse most of my freshman students.

a. ☐   timeworn classical syllogisms

b. ☐   complex mathematical proofs

c. ☐   Zen riddles designed to teach the inadequacy of logical reasoning

d. ☐   subtle paradoxes

e. ☐   examples of traditional Oriental wisdom

9. Scientists initially were astonished by the appearance of the **caldera.**

a. ☐   deep hole at the top of a volcano

b. ☐   black hole in a distant galaxy

c. ☐   polar ice formation

d. ☐   primitive cooking stove

e. ☐   heat source in ocean bottom

10. What I particularly admire are the **urceolate** forms the artist employs.

a. ☐   shaped like a bear

b. ☐   organic

c. ☐   free-flowing

d. ☐   irregularly patterned

e. ☐   shaped like an urn

■ *ZINGERS*

A. **usufruct:** the legal right to

a. ☐   assignment of ownership of property and any income it produces

b. ☐   enjoyment of use of property belonging to another person short of its destruction

c. ☐   unrestricted ownership of property and income produced during one's lifetime

d. ☐   restricted ownership of property but not the income produced

e. ☐   use of property jointly with heirs to an estate, with full ownership passing to the surviving partner

B. **tussive:** relating to

a. ☐   silk production

b. ☐   coughing

c. ☐   an inclination to struggle

d. ☐   cooperative effort

e. ☐   arctic terrain

Test
TWENTY-FOUR

1. The platform drafted last year did not reflect the views of **rabid** conservatives.

a. ☐   moderate

b. ☐   thoughtful

c. ☐   well-informed

d. ☐   fanatical

e. ☐   conventional

2. **Jocular** comments about absent members of the family were common at their dinner table.

a. ☐   gossipy

b. ☐   cruel

c. ☐   joking

d. ☐   critical

e. ☐   unflattering

3. It seemed to be his nature to **wallow** in accounts of the misfortunes of others.

a. ☐   accept without question

b. ☐   take unrestrained delight in

c. ☐ treat with unconcern

d. ☐ show concern for

e. ☐ treat with scorn

4. Voters will consider the mayor's program for housing the poor nothing more than transparent **trumpery.**

a. ☐ nonsense

b. ☐ futile dreaming

c. ☐ dishonesty

d. ☐ effort to placate critics

e. ☐ empty promise

5. O'Connor's **vignettes** demonstrated once again her outstanding ability as a writer of fiction.

a. ☐ brief narratives

b. ☐ character sketches

c. ☐ short novels

d. ☐ intricate plots

e. ☐ insights into motivations

6. Without a generous supply of **provender,** the expedition seemed doomed from the start.

a. ☐ medicine

b. ☐ merchandise for barter

c. ☐ equipment

d. ☐ tenting

e. ☐ fodder

7. In a few days the sores began to **suppurate.**

a. ☐ fester

b. ☐ worsen

c. ☐ darken

d. ☐ give pain

e. ☐ multiply

8. In her first attempt at woodworking, she managed to achieve the desired **marmoreal** finish.

a. ☐ shining

b. ☐ reflective

c. ☐ marble-like

d. ☐ multicolored

e. ☐ natural

9. The roofer was instructed to **imbricate** the shingles.

a. ☐ install in double thickness

b. ☐ overlap

c. ☐ apply waterproofing

d. ☐ inspect and repair

e. ☐ employ twice the usual number of nails

10. Her **onomastic** research was helped immeasurably by the library's recent acquisition of early American historical documents.

a. ☐ relating to word origins

b. ☐ relating to individual development

c. ☐ relating to names

d. ☐ relating to hierarchical institutions

e. ☐ relating to governmental policy

■ *ZINGERS*

A. **fulgurate:**

a. ☐ make sudden noises

b. ☐ praise extravagantly

   c. ☐   condemn vituperatively

   d. ☐   glow steadily

   e. ☐   emit flashes

B. doch-an-dorrach:

   a. ☐   parting drink

   b. ☐   mercy shown by victor to vanquished

   c. ☐   small gift offered at the start of the year

   d. ☐   brotherly love

   e. ☐   winner's prize in a contest of strength

Test
<u>TWENTY-FIVE</u>

1. Henri was able to put together an altogether pleasing **mélange** within a matter of minutes.

   a. ☐   mixture

   b. ☐   rich dessert

   c. ☐   omelet

   d. ☐   advertising layout

   e. ☐   cocktail

2. The scholar's **esoteric** presentation astounded the audience.

   a. ☐   of striking interest

   b. ☐   intended only for the initiated

   c. ☐   advanced in thought

   d. ☐   revolutionary in approach

   e. ☐   showing extreme confusion

3. Stealth is commonly agreed to be the **raison d'être** for the submarine.

   a. ☐ principal appeal

   b. ☐ underlying attraction

   c. ☐ main advantage

   d. ☐ reason for existing

   e. ☐ military purpose

4. She is said to have been the daughter of a **helot.**

   a. ☐ prostitute in ancient Greece

   b. ☐ member of the ruling class in ancient Rome

   c. ☐ Spartan serf

   d. ☐ Carthaginian warrior

   e. ☐ Roman gladiator

5. Seldom have we observed **alopecia** in a girl so young.

   a. ☐ extreme farsightedness

   b. ☐ generalized feebleness

   c. ☐ loss of hair

   d. ☐ sign of sexual maturity

   e. ☐ severe general neurological impairment

6. The disco quickly acquired a reputation for attracting **caparisoned** clientele.

   a. ☐ free-spending

   b. ☐ skilled in dancing

   c. ☐ showing taste in music

   d. ☐ freed of inhibition

   e. ☐ richly dressed

7. A man with mind made up on a question is, **a fortiori,** a man who can no longer reason objectively on it.

   a. ☐   for a stronger reason

   b. ☐   of logical advantage

   c. ☐   from then on

   d. ☐   as a consequence

   e. ☐   from the start

8. John tried as hard as he could but was unable to find a suitable **reticule.**

   a. ☐   prayer book

   b. ☐   monocular sight

   c. ☐   woman's handbag

   d. ☐   collection of proverbs

   e. ☐   type of inexpensive jewelry

9. We are told that **patchouli** is available here.

   a. ☐   type of herb

   b. ☐   type of incense

   c. ☐   type of ink

   d. ☐   type of candy

   e. ☐   type of perfume

10. His latest work in the theater has been termed **outré.**

   a. ☐   in the forefront of dramatic technique

   b. ☐   outside the bounds of what is considered proper

   c. ☐   excessively partisan in outlook

   d. ☐   out of the mainstream

   e. ☐   beyond the understanding of all but a select group

■ *ZINGERS*

A. **reredos:**

a. ☐ support for a weak back

b. ☐ type of tropical bat

c. ☐ ornamental altar screen

d. ☐ ornately carved bedpost

e. ☐ elaborate argument in rebuttal

B. **schwarmerei:**

a. ☐ inclination to daydream

b. ☐ extravagant enthusiasm

c. ☐ elaborate pastry

d. ☐ zealous advocacy

e. ☐ hopeless confusion

Test
TWENTY-SIX

1. Emma's colleagues gathered in the large hall in **homage** to her many achievements.

a. ☐ welcoming ceremony

b. ☐ things said as a mark of respect

c. ☐ overdue recognition

d. ☐ final tribute

e. ☐ undeserved compliments

2. Their lawyers claimed the confession was made under **duress.**

a. ☐ harsh conditions

b. ☐ agreement not to prosecute

c. ☐   use of force to procure something

d. ☐   illegal procedures

e. ☐   unfair procedures

3. His **foibles** were overlooked by the great majority of his patients.

a. ☐   errors of judgment

b. ☐   personal habits

c. ☐   persistent and annoying questions

d. ☐   harmless flaws in character

e. ☐   prying manners

4. The first problem faced by leaders is to arrange for the sort of **ordnance** that will be most helpful.

a. ☐   statute

b. ☐   procurement procedure

c. ☐   measuring device

d. ☐   military supplies

e. ☐   mathematical proof

5. Many political scientists have suggested that our government has become a **leviathan.**

a. ☐   something of enormous size

b. ☐   threat to survival

c. ☐   organization unresponsive to people's needs

d. ☐   body interested primarily in self-perpetuation

e. ☐   model for others to follow

6. Absence of a **caesura** went unnoticed.

a. ☐   earned military decoration

b. ☐   pause near the middle of a line of verse

c. ☐   device for performing an obstetrical procedure

d. ☐ device for aerating lawns

e. ☐ body of troops capable of making an assault

7. His knack for coming up with inappropriate **apothegms** accounts for his campus reputation.

a. ☐ swear words

b. ☐ words of encouragement

c. ☐ pithy sayings

d. ☐ descriptive words

e. ☐ elaborate metaphors

8. Much to my surprise, I found that he was known as an **ailurophile.**

a. ☐ collector of rare books

b. ☐ cat fancier

c. ☐ charitable person

d. ☐ trusting person

e. ☐ helpful person

9. That she was not guilty of **peculation** was obvious from the start.

a. ☐ sinful behavior

b. ☐ habitual lying

c. ☐ reckless investment of funds

d. ☐ embezzlement

e. ☐ habitual irritation

10. I soon tired of his **quiddities.**

a. ☐ trifling points

b. ☐ repeated suggestions

c. ☐ attempts to convince

d. ☐ requests for money

e. ☐ persistent attempts to make others look foolish

■ *ZINGERS*

A. **rimose:**

a. ☐ despairing

b. ☐ full of fissures

c. ☐ at the point of tears

d. ☐ teetering on the brink

e. ☐ branching in many directions

B. **rescission:**

a. ☐ repeated cutting

b. ☐ modification

c. ☐ severe editing

d. ☐ return of a manuscript

e. ☐ cancellation

Test
TWENTY-SEVEN

1. Committee leaders called for a vote on **impeachment.**

a. ☐ removal from office

b. ☐ acceptance of resignation of a government official

c. ☐ criminal charge of elected official

d. ☐ investigation of misconduct in office

e. ☐ accusation of treason or high crime

2. Over and over again, they studied every **facet** of the situation.

   a. ☐ intricacy

   b. ☐ possible cause

   c. ☐ aspect

   d. ☐ possible result

   e. ☐ important factor

3. Despite everything we tried, we could not overcome the **lassitude** that had afflicted us for more than a week.

   a. ☐ feeling of suspicion

   b. ☐ listlessness

   c. ☐ weakness

   d. ☐ emotional shock

   e. ☐ deep-seated anxiety

4. Nurses reported that **edema** became more pronounced as the night wore on.

   a. ☐ difficulty in breathing

   b. ☐ elevation in body temperature

   c. ☐ color change in part of the body

   d. ☐ abnormal retention of body fluid

   e. ☐ symptom of congestive heart failure

5. Although the poet was afflicted with **amblyopia** from late adolescence until the end of his life, he never let the condition impede his work.

   a. ☐ double vision

   b. ☐ extreme nearsightedness

   c. ☐ impaired vision without apparent change in the eyes

   d. ☐ extreme farsightedness

   e. ☐ severe astigmatism

6. The group stopped to examine a **campanile** of extraordinary beauty.

   a. ☐ bell tower

   b. ☐ type of flowering plant

   c. ☐ waterfall

   d. ☐ grassy plain

   e. ☐ early fortress

7. We spent most of our time working on the many **frangible** items she had collected over her lifetime.

   a. ☐ extremely valuable

   b. ☐ breakable

   c. ☐ beautiful

   d. ☐ illegally procured

   e. ☐ procured at low cost

8. Most of Ray's associates considered him an extraordinary **pettifogger.**

   a. ☐ quibbler

   b. ☐ local meteorologist

   c. ☐ attorney specializing in public advocacy

   d. ☐ petty thief

   e. ☐ complete scoundrel

9. Professor Slade spent most of her summer studying the **littoral.**

   a. ☐ verbatim translation of a text

   b. ☐ rite prescribed for public worship

   c. ☐ region lying along a shore

   d. ☐ primitive form of worship

   e. ☐ layer of stone and rock

10. I would rather give up my personal computer than do without the **vade mecum** my grandfather gave me.

   a. ☐   versatile tool

   b. ☐   book for ready reference

   c. ☐   carry-all

   d. ☐   unabridged dictionary

   e. ☐   perpetual calendar

◼ *ZINGERS*

A. **sciolist:**

   a. ☐   person who incorrectly applies the scientific method

   b. ☐   annotator of difficult texts

   c. ☐   charlatan who claims to call forth the spirits of the dead

   d. ☐   superficial pretender to knowledge

   e. ☐   pedantic scholar

B. **telic:**

   a. ☐   directed to a definite end

   b. ☐   intended to expand or explain

   c. ☐   lacking element needed for completion

   d. ☐   intended to explain natural phenomena

   e. ☐   made and abandoned by early humans

Test
TWENTY-EIGHT

1. Once again, and predictably, the unrestrained enthusiasm Kate mustered for her plan **engendered** apathy in the rest of us.

   a. ☐ gave rise to

   b. ☐ overcame

   c. ☐ increased

   d. ☐ substantially reinforced

   e. ☐ accounted for

2. Are you certain the problem is within his **bailiwick?**

   a. ☐ level of competency

   b. ☐ financial means

   c. ☐ sphere of operations

   d. ☐ professional judgment

   e. ☐ professional qualifications

3. Strange to say, the miniseries provided a profound **catharsis** for many viewers.

   a. ☐ feeling of extreme revulsion

   b. ☐ welcome understanding of one's heritage

   c. ☐ insight into problems common to most people

   d. ☐ insight into psychological problems faced by one's family

   e. ☐ purification of emotions through viewing art

4. It was many years before she was able to live down her well-deserved reputation as a **hoyden.**

   a. ☐ unnaturally reserved woman

   b. ☐ promiscuous woman

   c. ☐ boisterous girl

d. ☐   ringleader in all pranks

e. ☐   hostile person

5. Scholars considered the **distaff** side of his family by far the more interesting.

a. ☐   immigrant

b. ☐   female

c. ☐   inclined to intellectual life

d. ☐   distantly related

e. ☐   occupied with manual labor

6. The director puzzled long over the challenge of preserving sympathy for a character whose every line of reasoning was clearly **meretricious.**

a. ☐   exhibiting hostility

b. ☐   flaunting a sense of righteousness

c. ☐   conveying the appearance of intellectual superiority

d. ☐   based on insincerity

e. ☐   displaying arrogance

7. Anna made it clear a **palfry** no longer interested her.

a. ☐   saddle horse suitable for a woman

b. ☐   small increase in salary

c. ☐   session of small talk

d. ☐   life as an artist

e. ☐   career without management responsibility or recognition

8. Ireland still offers the visitor the chance to see a **dolmen,** especially in unspoiled rural areas.

a. ☐   prehistoric structure with flat stone laid on upright stones

b. ☐   narrow window typically found in ancient castles

   c. ☐   woman's dress having very wide sleeves but tight at the wrists

   d. ☐   thatched cottage consisting of a single large room

   e. ☐   peat bog

9. Atkins made her reputation as a specialist in **ramose** coral structures.

   a. ☐   infrequently encountered

   b. ☐   branching

   c. ☐   classical

   d. ☐   rapidly growing

   e. ☐   extremely complex and challenging

10. The youth's **temerarious** behavior during the events leading up to the tragedy went unnoticed in the police reports.

   a. ☐   uncooperative

   b. ☐   rash

   c. ☐   uncommonly brave

   d. ☐   revealing fright

   e. ☐   marked by secrecy

■   *ZINGERS*

A. **autochthonous:**

   a. ☐   self-righteous

   b. ☐   pervading all phases of life

   c. ☐   indigenous

   d. ☐   independent of foreign sources

   e. ☐   derived from the same source

B. **tomentose:**

a. ☐ long-suffering

b. ☐ closely covered with thick hair

c. ☐ deprived of external stimuli

d. ☐ tumescent

e. ☐ convoluted

Test
<u>TWENTY-NINE</u>

1. Support by the same small group of **bovine** politicians did little for the bill.

a. ☐ petty

b. ☐ undistinguished

c. ☐ dull and stupid

d. ☐ of extreme views

e. ☐ coming from agricultural regions

2. The presidential aide **feigned** ignorance of the great number of illegal acts that occurred during his early days in the administration.

a. ☐ pleaded

b. ☐ maintained

c. ☐ obscured

d. ☐ pretended

e. ☐ revealed

3. To some it was a **nettlesome** situation that soon enough would surely resolve itself.

a. ☐ temporary

b. ☐ causing annoyance

c. ☐ demanding courage

d. ☐ harmful

e. ☐ testing faith

4. The knights agreed to **joust** during the tournament.

a. ☐ engage in personal combat

b. ☐ seek official permission

c. ☐ settle a dispute fairly

d. ☐ ask for exoneration

e. ☐ reaffirm allegiance

5. Last year's summit meeting opened with a Soviet **gambit** so unexpected that a two-week adjournment was immediately requested.

a. ☐ incomprehensible offer

b. ☐ generous offer to settle outstanding disputes

c. ☐ openly hostile action

d. ☐ statement intended to secure an advantage

e. ☐ display of cooperative behavior

6. Showing **diffidence** during a job interview can be expected to affect an applicant's chances.

a. ☐ awkwardness in speech

b. ☐ appropriate assertiveness

c. ☐ excessive shyness

d. ☐ politeness

e. ☐ respect for another

7. I counted twelve examples of **tautology** in a single page of his speech.

a. ☐ disagreement of antecedent and pronoun

b. ☐ stylistic fault of saying same thing twice in different words

c. ☐   lack of coherence in writing

d. ☐   inappropriately flowery expression

e. ☐   inappropriate mixture of active and passive constructions

8. Saturday night entertainment at the White House is not to be thought of as a **saturnalia.**

   a. ☐   time of quiet enjoyment

   b. ☐   time for paying political debts

   c. ☐   period of religious devotion

   d. ☐   time of wild revelry

   e. ☐   occasion for celebration of the performing arts

9. Her **lugubrious** expression clearly signaled I was to watch my every action that morning.

   a. ☐   hostile

   b. ☐   angry

   c. ☐   sly

   d. ☐   determined

   e. ☐   dismal

10. Once again he felt **crapulous,** the familiar condition telling him he could not bear to face work that day.

   a. ☐   vaguely uncomfortable

   b. ☐   sick from excessive drinking

   c. ☐   chronically complaining

   d. ☐   perceiving persistent pain in the bowel

   e. ☐   unable to rouse enthusiasm

■ *ZINGERS*

A. **ophidian:** relating to

a. ☐ spiders

b. ☐ snakes

c. ☐ gems

d. ☐ multiple deities

e. ☐ creatures of the sea

B. **ratiné:**

a. ☐ plan incorporating multiple elements

b. ☐ dish of noodles covered with melted cheese

c. ☐ fabric of nubby yarns

d. ☐ lacelike pattern

e. ☐ mixture of dissimilar elements

Test
THIRTY

1. Even in the act of dying, Alan showed characteristic **bravado.**

a. ☐ allegiance to duty

b. ☐ pretense of boldness

c. ☐ true brilliance as a thinker

d. ☐ faithfulness to friends

e. ☐ personal courage

2. Good intentions forgotten, the three members of the senator's staff accused one another of **unconscionable** acts.

a. ☐ contrary to what one's conscience knows is right

b. ☐ contrary to what one expects of public servants

c. ☐ contrary to prevailing concepts of morality

d. ☐ contrary to public policy

e. ☐ contrary to prevailing civil or criminal law

3. With death fast approaching, he expressed regret that he still had not made the **hajj.**

a. ☐ peace with Allah

b. ☐ Muslim form of last will and testament

c. ☐ holy war

d. ☐ pilgrimage to Mecca

e. ☐ arrangement for marriage of a daughter in the Muslim tradition

4. Only her closest friends knew her for the **harridan** she had become.

a. ☐ harassed person

b. ☐ victim of a sadistic husband

c. ☐ object of pity or scorn

d. ☐ penniless person

e. ☐ bad-tempered old woman

5. Stories of his behavior during his middle years reflected the **epiphany** he experienced during his long illness.

a. ☐ complete devastation of the central nervous system

b. ☐ virtual destruction of the digestive tract

c. ☐ sudden, intuitive perception of the essential meaning of something

d. ☐ extensive vascular damage

e. ☐ extraordinary review of one's past life leading to complete change of behavior

6. She is at her best as **soubrette** in the operas of Puccini.

 a. ☐ seductress

 b. ☐ woman who loves but is not loved in return

 c. ☐ tragic heroine

 d. ☐ frivolous young woman

 e. ☐ young woman doomed to disappointment in life

7. A second examination revealed that the **buccal** cavity was the principal site of infection.

 a. ☐ relating to the anus

 b. ☐ relating to the nose

 c. ☐ relating to the mouth

 d. ☐ relating to the ear

 e. ☐ relating to the intestines

8. **Distichous** leaves are typically found in plants of that class.

 a. ☐ having two lobes

 b. ☐ arranged in two vertical rows

 c. ☐ arranged in two horizontal rows

 d. ☐ appearing twice each year

 e. ☐ having flattened stems

9. Paleontologists described the creature as **soricine** in most respects.

 a. ☐ adapted for foraging underground

 b. ☐ living in small family groups

 c. ☐ showing signs of sisterly behavior

 d. ☐ resembling the shrews

 e. ☐ adapted for living in deserts

10. Even as a child, Schmidt had been **froward,** arrogant, and delightfully mischievous.

a. ☐   difficult to deal with

b. ☐   open in manner

c. ☐   outspoken

d. ☐   secretive

e. ☐   inclined to speak one's mind

■   *ZINGERS*

A. **vagile:**

a. ☐   ineffectual

b. ☐   indistinctly perceived

c. ☐   free to move about

d. ☐   easily replaceable

e. ☐   sheathlike

B. **telamon:** male figure used as

a. ☐   supporting column

b. ☐   artist's model

c. ☐   ornamentation

d. ☐   object of worship

e. ☐   representation of virility

Test
THIRTY-ONE

1. His **yeoman** service to the law firm went unrecognized until after his death.

   a. ☐ long and faithful

   b. ☐ discreet

   c. ☐ poorly paid

   d. ☐ outstanding

   e. ☐ useful and quiet

2. Sir William is an eminent **barrister.**

   a. ☐ chief legal advisor to county governments in Great Britain

   b. ☐ prosecutor in courts of Great Britain

   c. ☐ lawyer representing clients in higher law courts of Great Britain

   d. ☐ lawyer who prepares law cases for presentation by solicitors in Great Britain

   e. ☐ legal advisor to British royal family

3. Not one of us could recall ever seeing him without a **cheroot.**

   a. ☐ cigar open at both ends

   b. ☐ set of Muslim prayer beads

   c. ☐ good luck charm

   d. ☐ matched pair of steel balls

   e. ☐ knife for whittling

4. **Abstemious** people generally outlive those who indulge freely.

   a. ☐ abstaining completely from alcoholic drinks

   b. ☐ careful with money

   c. ☐ disciplined to eat at regular intervals

d. ☐   sparing in taking food and drink

e. ☐   eating only healthful foods

5. Two of the sorority sisters interviewing Jenny found her **didactic.**

a. ☐   offensively prudish

b. ☐   having the manner of one who is lecturing pupils

c. ☐   cooperative and respectful

d. ☐   completely uncompromising in opinions

e. ☐   thoughtful in answering questions

6. Henry found himself uncomfortable in the role of faithful **acolyte** and longed for the day when his situation would change.

a. ☐   person not expected to offer opinions

b. ☐   apprentice carpenter

c. ☐   eldest son

d. ☐   editorial assistant

e. ☐   attendant or junior assistant

7. The **catafalque** finally made its long-awaited appearance.

a. ☐   ceremonial cannon

b. ☐   twin-hulled boat

c. ☐   structure for carrying a coffin

d. ☐   complete edition of an author's work

e. ☐   elaborate model used to plan full-scale manufacture

8. **Sutlers** fulfilled an essential function in the operations of Union armies west of the Mississippi.

a. ☐   provisioners

b. ☐   scouts

c. ☐   rifle repairmen

d. ☐ undercover agents

e. ☐ artillery officers

9. The **voir dire** was scheduled for the next day.

a. ☐ conference called before sentencing by a judge

b. ☐ application for termination of a court case

c. ☐ preliminary examination of a witness or juror

d. ☐ hearing contemplating suspension of jury deliberations

e. ☐ opportunity for presenting preliminary arguments by attorneys in a case

10. A great number of scholars have found the **uncial** difficult to interpret.

a. ☐ predominant orthodox teaching

b. ☐ inscribed stone

c. ☐ ancient ceremonial procedure

d. ☐ style of manuscript writing

e. ☐ system of encoding messages

■ *ZINGERS*

A. **vaticinate:**

a. ☐ waver

b. ☐ prophesy

c. ☐ rationalize

d. ☐ correct

e. ☐ improve

B. **tropophilous:** adapted to a climate that is

a. ☐ uniformly wet and hot

b. ☐ uniformly wet and cold

c. ☐ uniformly dry and cold

d. ☐ uniformly dry and hot

e. ☐ alternately wet and cold and dry and hot

Test
THIRTY-TWO

1. For Kate's birthday, Michael bought her a **bauble** she cherished more than any present he had given her previously.

a. ☐ sentimental gift

b. ☐ showy ornament of little value

c. ☐ engraved art work

d. ☐ ancient oil lamp

e. ☐ antique ring

2. They managed to secure a **lectern** just in time for the opening session.

a. ☐ speaker's platform

b. ☐ reading light for a speaker

c. ☐ stand designed to hold text for a speaker

d. ☐ public address system

e. ☐ sounding board above or behind a public speaker

3. As Charles aged, he grew increasingly **incontinent.**

a. ☐ lacking in judgment

b. ☐ intolerant

c. ☐ sharp in criticism

d. ☐ lacking in self-restraint

e. ☐ forgetful

4. Many Soviet officials acquire a **dacha** when they advance in seniority.

  a. ☐ small country house

  b. ☐ private secretary

  c. ☐ private office

  d. ☐ automobile

  e. ☐ permit to shop in stores intended primarily for foreigners

5. Needless to say, the **cabochon** worn by the dean's wife attracted much attention at the faculty party.

  a. ☐ polished unfaceted gem

  b. ☐ diamond necklace

  c. ☐ dress with low-cut neckline

  d. ☐ formal gown

  e. ☐ gem of great value

6. Much to my surprise, I found her ideas refreshingly **eclectic.**

  a. ☐ suitable for all tastes

  b. ☐ carefully conforming to prevailing opinion

  c. ☐ drawn freely from various sources

  d. ☐ unconventional

  e. ☐ easy to comprehend and explain to others

7. Instead of the **exegesis** we had anticipated, we were treated to a bitter attack on the practices of book reviewers.

  a. ☐ reading of one's own literary work

  b. ☐ critical interpretation

  c. ☐ brilliant sermon

  d. ☐ personal reminiscence

  e. ☐ encouraging message or lesson

8. More promising **juvenilia** have yet to be found.

   a. ☐ young people

   b. ☐ programs intended to help adolescents develop normally

   c. ☐ foods and drugs intended to restore youthful vigor

   d. ☐ courses intended for young people

   e. ☐ works produced by an author or artist in youth

9. In his eyes we were the **canaille** and were treated appropriately.

   a. ☐ people of talent

   b. ☐ troublemakers

   c. ☐ people given to telling lies

   d. ☐ artists and writers

   e. ☐ riffraff

10. A **gonfalon** on exhibition at the Metropolitan Museum of Art is considered an excellent example of medieval Italian work.

   a. ☐ neckpiece made of silver and gold

   b. ☐ banner hanging from a frame

   c. ☐ tapestry depicting scenes of martyrdom

   d. ☐ ornately carved children's bed

   e. ☐ intricate work by a goldsmith

■ *ZINGERS*

A. **nautch:**

   a. ☐ species of tropical freshwater fish

   b. ☐ academic certificate equivalent to teacher's license

   c. ☐ Indian entertainment featuring dancing girls

   d. ☐ species of mollusk

   e. ☐ outer garment worn by Muslim women

B. **paillette:**

a. ☐   pointed spear intended for use in piercing armor
b. ☐   camper's inflatable pillow
c. ☐   long stake used in making fencing
d. ☐   small shiny object
e. ☐   article made of straw

Test
THIRTY-THREE

1. Obviously, the real purpose of the meeting was to **foment** trouble within the department.

a. ☐   prevent
b. ☐   instigate
c. ☐   patch up
d. ☐   reduce
e. ☐   increase

2. I am certain they will find it easier to **capitulate** once they fully understand the situation.

a. ☐   agree
b. ☐   cooperate
c. ☐   surrender
d. ☐   merge
e. ☐   secure financing

3. All the signs of **decadence** were present even though few of us could recognize them.

a. ☐   period of decline
b. ☐   end of an era

c. ☐ new society

d. ☐ conditions for rapid growth

e. ☐ revolution

4. There is no doubt that an ability to listen closely is the **cachet** of a first-class conversationalist.

a. ☐ trade secret

b. ☐ most important technique

c. ☐ distinguishing feature

d. ☐ hidden trait

e. ☐ trick

5. His **baleful** glances had their intended effect.

a. ☐ lovesick

b. ☐ piteous

c. ☐ ominous

d. ☐ imploring

e. ☐ made in an open manner

6. The fact that Will's remarks usually are perceived as clever but not **apposite** bothers him not at all.

a. ☐ effective as rebuttal

b. ☐ worth repeating

c. ☐ clearly thought out

d. ☐ appropriate for a purpose

e. ☐ of great importance

7. Buchwald's latest column on the antics of baseball stars was considered **lese majesty** by fans who take the game too seriously.

a. ☐ deliberate insult

b. ☐ presumptuous behavior

   c. □   undeserved mockery

   d. □   criticism based on lack of understanding

   e. □   harmless fun

8. The **intrados** typically comprises seven smoothly finished stones.

   a. □   inside curve of an arch

   b. □   section of vaulted ceiling of a chapel

   c. □   section of floor of a transept

   d. □   rear portion of a chapel

   e. □   floor of entrance to a chancel

9. Recent years have seen the **apotheosis** of the office of president.

   a. □   virtual destruction

   b. □   gradual weakening

   c. □   increased use of power

   d. □   elevation to godly status

   e. □   clear definition of power

10. She used a **heuristic** computer program to identify the elements of her problem requiring better definition.

   a. □   of great complexity

   b. □   incorporating many small steps

   c. □   requiring greater than usual capacity

   d. □   proceeding by trial and error

   e. □   well defined

■ *ZINGERS*

A. **noetic:**

a. ☐   purely abstract or intellectual

b. ☐   based on perception by the five senses

c. ☐   based on intuition

d. ☐   employing experience alone

e. ☐   following established mathematical reasoning

B. **intaglio:** a type of carving in stone or other hard material in which the design is

a. ☐   produced by cutting away all the material except for the design, which is left intact

b. ☐   lightly cut into the surface and completed by etching

c. ☐   cut into the surface, leaving the remaining material untouched

d. ☐   cut into the surface and then filled with enamel of various colors

e. ☐   cut into the surface and then filled with lead before polishing

Test
THIRTY-FOUR

1. Eric's behavior made it clear he looked upon himself as a sort of **vizier.**

a. ☐   financial wizard

b. ☐   minister of state

c. ☐   prophet

d. ☐   know-it-all

e. ☐   gift to mankind

2. Once the governor **recanted,** the judge decided to declare a mistrial.

a. ☐   refused to testify

b. ☐   challenged authority of the court

c. ☐   disavowed an earlier statement

d. ☐   claimed executive privilege

e. ☐   refused to take an oath

3. **Unrestrained** growth marked the city's early years.

a. ☐   very rapid

b. ☐   uncontrolled

c. ☐   unpredictable

d. ☐   immeasurable

e. ☐   excessive

4. The entire neighborhood spoke of Rebecca's **winsome** manner.

a. ☐   charming and attractive

b. ☐   tending to promote success

c. ☐   marked by constant complaint

d. ☐   distant and forbidding

e. ☐   insincere and seductive

5. Long, **turbid** responses by the principal defense witness caused great concern about the effect of her testimony.

a. ☐   evasive

b. ☐   incomplete

c. ☐   hostile

d. ☐   confused

e. ☐   giving the impression of lying

6. The veterinarian failed to examine the **withers** thoroughly before declaring that the horse was sound.

   a. ☐   buttocks of a horse

   b. ☐   thigh of a horse

   c. ☐   shoulders of a horse

   d. ☐   ridge between the shoulder blades of a horse

   e. ☐   forearm, elbow, and knee of a horse

7. Tanaka took great pleasure in showing visitors his outstanding collection of **kakemonos.**

   a. ☐   long Japanese gowns

   b. ☐   erotic Japanese paintings

   c. ☐   Japanese fans

   d. ☐   Japanese screens

   e. ☐   Japanese vertical hanging scrolls

8. Life with a **punctilious** husband is not always easy.

   a. ☐   obsessively punctual

   b. ☐   attentive to details of conduct

   c. ☐   overly careful in matters of personal hygiene

   d. ☐   demanding constant attention

   e. ☐   showing jealousy

9. The court concerned itself principally with whether the author intended to write primarily for the **prurient** reader.

   a. ☐   given to lascivious desires

   b. ☐   given to appropriate modesty

   c. ☐   given to prudent behavior

   d. ☐   entirely moral

   e. ☐   sufficiently mature

10. Before Dr. Forman turned to **nosology,** she had been recognized by her associates as an outstanding pediatric surgeon.

a. ☐ plastic surgery

b. ☐ tropical medicine

c. ☐ classification of diseases

d. ☐ study of fetal development

e. ☐ study of unconventional medical treatment

■ *ZINGERS*

A. **cicatrix:**

a. ☐ guide

b. ☐ scar

c. ☐ lover

d. ☐ insect

e. ☐ liar

B. **anadiplosis:**

a. ☐ repeated use of two or more pairs of grammatically similar words within a sentence

b. ☐ repeated use of a striking word or phrase within a sentence

c. ☐ sudden interruption of a thought by a speaker to convey unwillingness or inability to continue

d. ☐ repetition of a concluding or prominent word of a sentence or clause at the beginning of the next

e. ☐ repetition of a word or phrase at the beginnings of two or more consecutive clauses or verses

Test
THIRTY-FIVE

1. The **myriad** problems we face can be solved, if at all, only by extraordinary cooperative effort.

   a. □ of great complexity

   b. □ personal in nature

   c. □ indefinitely great in number

   d. □ demanding individual attention by skilled workers

   e. □ deep and persistent

2. It was obvious from the start that the dean would be **loath** to fulfill her promises.

   a. □ reluctant

   b. □ unable

   c. □ slow

   d. □ forbidden

   e. □ inclined

3. We were looking for a **factotum** willing to work for just a little more than the minimum wage.

   a. □ unskilled domestic worker

   b. □ foreign girl working as a domestic and treated as a member of the employer's family

   c. □ apprentice bookkeeper

   d. □ person who does all kinds of work

   e. □ person skilled in all the building trades

4. Great numbers of unhappy adolescents were attracted by promises of **nirvana** in ten easy lessons.

   a. □ moral and physical perfection

   b. □ psychic well-being

c. ☐   freedom from the external world

d. ☐   continuing exuberance

e. ☐   keen perception of reality

5. For their wedding anniversary he bought his wife a necklace of **baroque** pearls.

a. ☐   dating from the 17th century

b. ☐   imported from the Orient

c. ☐   of uniform size and shape

d. ☐   natural rather than cultured

e. ☐   irregular in shape

6. His **cant** fooled nobody but the portion of the television audience that consistently supported him.

a. ☐   political or social bias

b. ☐   insincere use of words suggesting piety

c. ☐   tendency to exaggerate

d. ☐   promises made without intention to fulfill them

e. ☐   line of patter

7. Progress of the species was **saltatory,** according to Darwin.

a. ☐   proceeding by abrupt movements

b. ☐   slow and steady

c. ☐   encouraged by changes in the environment

d. ☐   in the direction of specialization

e. ☐   helpful for the environment

8. What the project needed but never found was an effective **oriflamme.**

a. ☐   rallying point

b. ☐   ample source of fuel

c. ☐   pilot light

d. ☐   source of dyes

e. ☐   overall plan of operation

9. Small **rasorial** birds became his particular interest.

a. ☐   adapted for seizing prey

b. ☐   given to scratching the ground for food

c. ☐   feeding on crawling insects and larva

d. ☐   feeding on nectar and pollen

e. ☐   feeding on fish and flying insects

10. Once I was perceived as a **quidnunc,** my future in the organization was doomed.

a. ☐   habitual exaggerator

b. ☐   prophet of doom

c. ☐   busybody

d. ☐   unproductive person

e. ☐   informer

■   *ZINGERS*

A. **orthoepy:**

a. ☐   remedial treatment of eye muscles

b. ☐   correction of misalignment of jaws

c. ☐   study of correct pronunciation

d. ☐   support of weak muscles

e. ☐   realignment of structures after damage

B. **jongleur:**

a. ☐   person whose speech is difficult to understand

b. ☐   jack-of-all-trades

c. ☐   unmitigated rogue

d. ☐   wandering minstrel

e. ☐   complete bungler

Test
THIRTY-SIX

1. As a result of governmental inaction, dozens of innovative programs lay **fallow.**

a. ☐   ready for prompt introduction

b. ☐   unappreciated by all but the most perceptive

c. ☐   gathering dust

d. ☐   potentially useful but not yet in use

e. ☐   untested

2. After a short time, even Bavarian whipped cream may **cloy.**

a. ☐   fail to satisfy

b. ☐   appear commonplace

c. ☐   become distasteful through overabundance

d. ☐   liquefy

e. ☐   spoil

3. Observers feared that the revolutionary **juggernaut** would crush all republican opposition.

a. ☐   cruel system of retribution

b. ☐   arbitrary tribunal

c. ☐   repressive government

d. ☐   underground movement

e. ☐   massive overpowering force

4. Admirers **beleaguered** Graham after her recital reached its triumphal conclusion.

   a. □ showered with flowers

   b. □ applauded vigorously

   c. □ voiced acclaim

   d. □ besieged

   e. □ showed love for

5. Late in his life, the **acrophobia** that long had handicapped him seemed suddenly to be manageable.

   a. □ abnormal fear of being at great heights

   b. □ abnormal fear of forming close friendships

   c. □ abnormal fear of handling animals

   d. □ abnormal fear of being in open spaces

   e. □ abnormal fear of being in crowds

6. With the passing of the **calumet,** the convocation officially ended.

   a. □ holy scripture

   b. □ wine decanter

   c. □ eucharistic cup

   d. □ crucifix

   e. □ Indian ceremonial pipe

7. **Contumely** became more and more frequent as the filibuster went into its third day.

   a. □ display of resentment

   b. □ reproachful language

   c. □ resort to pettiness

   d. □ exploitation of loopholes in procedural rules

   e. □ deft political maneuvering

8. The candidate was told that **perfervid** attacks directed at political opponents repel as many voters as they attract.

   a. □ vicious

   b. □ baseless

   c. □ very ardent

   d. □ poorly thought out

   e. □ personal

9. Until well into the morning of the second day, **rime** obscured
the enemy encampment.

   a. □ low-lying cloud cover

   b. □ dense fog

   c. ⊔ steady rainfall

   d. □ hoarfrost

   e. □ smokescreen

10. His **sempiternal** cynicism did little to endear him to those who
would normally have become his strongest supporters.

   a. □ annoying

   b. □ everlasting

   c. □ justifiable

   d. □ recurrent

   e. □ increasing

■ ZINGERS

A. **hidrosis:**

   a. □ drowning

   b. □ excessive loss of body fluid

   c. □ condition of marked loss of strength

   d. □ sweating

   e. □ dropsy

B. **prescind:**

a. ☐   give early permission

b. ☐   cut off abruptly

c. ☐   perceive before becoming fully aware

d. ☐   act to create a division in sentiment

e. ☐   deny permission to make application

Test
THIRTY-SEVEN

1. What we had in mind was a suitable **repast** to celebrate the team's great victory.

a. ☐   alcoholic drink

b. ☐   meal

c. ☐   prayer of thanksgiving

d. ☐   medallion

e. ☐   meeting

2. To be considered for full membership in the order, an applicant must spend at least two years as a **mendicant** in the streets of the city.

a. ☐   beggar

b. ☐   preacher

c. ☐   homeless person

d. ☐   social worker

e. ☐   person practicing total silence

3. Mark appeared so gaunt and **hirsute** that even close friends in the search party had difficulty in identifying him.

a. ☐   unkempt

b. ☐   changed in appearance

c. ☐ enfeebled

d. ☐ hairy

e. ☐ deeply burned by the sun

4. He knew at that moment that his **palmy** days were behind him from then on.

a. ☐ fondly recalled

b. ☐ marked by openness of mind and spirit

c. ☐ carefree

d. ☐ marked by challenges

e. ☐ prosperous

5. Several conferences were called to discuss the **etiology** of pancreatic cancer.

a. ☐ cause of a disease

b. ☐ treatment of a disease

c. ☐ predicted outcome of a disease

d. ☐ projection of life expectancy after contracting a disease

e. ☐ role of viral infection in a disease

6. We soon learned to take his **ex cathedra** pronouncements with a grain of salt.

a. ☐ unorthodox

b. ☐ authoritative

c. ☐ made without support of the church

d. ☐ of major importance

e. ☐ of minor importance

7. Once again her **casuistry** succeeded in swaying a majority of voters.

a. ☐ expert analysis of causes and effects

b. ☐ eloquent oratory

c. ☐ fallacious application of principles

d. ☐ habit of offering easy explanations for difficult problems

e. ☐ easygoing manner

8. The **rochet** occasioned a great deal of favorable comment in the crowded vestry.

a. ☐ example of 18th-century ecclesiastic art

b. ☐ staff resembling a shepherd's crook

c. ☐ finger ring worn as symbol of ecclesiastic authority

d. ☐ silver sacramental vessel

e. ☐ vestment worn especially by bishops

9. He owes his well-deserved notoriety to an unsurpassed gift for **scabrous** literary criticism.

a. ☐ nastily abusive

b. ☐ embarrassingly perceptive

c. ☐ gentle but perceptive

d. ☐ straightforward

e. ☐ realistic and well expressed

10. The great **anabasis** was celebrated by poets and historians.

a. ☐ war of independence of a people

b. ☐ difficult military retreat

c. ☐ religious revival

d. ☐ invasion of a foreign country

e. ☐ peace treaty

■ *ZINGERS*

A. **himation:** ancient Greek outer garment worn

a. ☐ by married women

b. ☐ over left shoulder and under right

119

   c. ☐ over both shoulders

   d. ☐ by virgins

   e. ☐ over right shoulder and under left

B. **oubliette:**

   a. ☐ louvered window blind

   b. ☐ window shade impenetrable to light

   c. ☐ dungeon with entrance only at top

   d. ☐ windowless room in a castle

   e. ☐ state of forgetfulness

Test
THIRTY-EIGHT

1. Mere addition of a few **filberts** improved the dish subtly.

   a. ☐ rare spices

   b. ☐ strips of boned fish

   c. ☐ hazelnuts

   d. ☐ blanched turnips

   e. ☐ apple slices

2. After performances, Cynthia usually met with other **balleto-manes** to chew over every aspect of what they had seen.

   a. ☐ amateur critics of ballet

   b. ☐ persons who attend ballet performances

   c. ☐ choreographers

   d. ☐ composers of music for the ballet

   e. ☐ ballet enthusiasts

3. My wife and I, try as we might, found no way to halt the developing **impasse.**

   a. □   general apathy

   b. □   deadlock

   c. □   threat of breakup of a marriage

   d. □   divergence of views

   e. □   threat of bankruptcy

4. Resplendent in his multicolored **dashiki,** Julian was the hit of the party.

   a. □   close-fitting jacket with high collar

   b. □   Muslim headdress

   c. □   potentate's formal costume

   d. □   loose-fitting pullover shirt

   e. □   East Indian robe

5. The **ferruginous** landscape has been captured many times by keen-eyed photographers.

   a. □   bright enough to dazzle the viewer

   b. □   reddish brown

   c. □   showing many shades of green

   d. □   slashed by mining operations

   e. □   multicolored

6. Computer-driven machines now can be used for supplying **hachures.**

   a. □   complex outline drawings that depict three-dimensional objects

   b. □   precise commands for milling metals

   c. □   lines used for shading in maps

   d. □   accurate sizes for manufactured components

   e. □   instructions in everyday language

7. **Feral** man has long intrigued the general public as well as many educational psychologists.

    a. ☐   resembling a wild animal

    b. ☐   unable to read or write

    c. ☐   primitive

    d. ☐   living in a hunting and gathering society

    e. ☐   completely free of inhibition

8. The **cenacle** stood on the top of the highest peak in our area.

    a. ☐   military observation tower

    b. ☐   astronomical observatory

    c. ☐   house used for religious retreat

    d. ☐   forest fire observation tower

    e. ☐   weather station

9. As far as is known, **loess** cannot be found anywhere in the eastern part of your state.

    a. ☐   deposit of sandstone

    b. ☐   mixture of sand and gravel

    c. ☐   heavy clay soil

    d. ☐   naturally occurring fossil remains

    e. ☐   unstratified loamy deposit

10. One of our reasons for making the trip was to witness an **eisteddfod.**

    a. ☐   celebration of Celtic language and religion

    b. ☐   Welsh gathering for competitions

    c. ☐   commemoration of original settlement of the British Isles

    d. ☐   Scandinavian athletic festival

    e. ☐   Icelandic celebration of the longest day of the year

■ *ZINGERS*

A. **muezzin:**

a. ☐ pilgrim retracing Muhammad's flight from Mecca

b. ☐ person dedicated to holy war on behalf of Islam

c. ☐ convert to Islam

d. ☐ person adhering to teachings of Sunni Muslim sect

e. ☐ Muslim crier who announces hours of prayer

B. **nevus:**

a. ☐ membrane-covered opening in bone

b. ☐ irregular red birthmark

c. ☐ title of sovereign of Ethiopia

d. ☐ infant drawing first breaths after birth

e. ☐ symbol used in notation of Gregorian chant

Test
THIRTY-NINE

1. Not unexpectedly, a **wayward** son often becomes everyone's favorite within a family.

a. ☐ disobedient

b. ☐ self-reliant

c. ☐ submissive

d. ☐ ambitious

e. ☐ strong-willed

2. Never for a moment did Jack **rue** the day he asked you to marry him.

a. ☐ forget

b. ☐ take notice of

c. ☐ regret

d. ☐ look back on

e. ☐ recall

3.   **Zealots** in his own party took the lead in opposing the president's foreign policy.

a. ☐ self-seeking persons

b. ☐ left-wingers

c. ☐ fair-weather friends

d. ☐ right-wingers

e. ☐ extreme partisans

4. In the bottle that stood on the night table, only a single **troche** remained of the twenty-five originally purchased.

a. ☐ capsule

b. ☐ painkiller

c. ☐ lozenge

d. ☐ headache powder

e. ☐ sleeping pill

5. Before pronouncing sentence, the judge dwelled at length on the **enormity** of the crime for which the convicted person was to be punished.

a. ☐ incurable nature

b. ☐ true motive

c. ☐ manner of commission

d. ☐ monstrous wickedness

e. ☐ extraordinary nature

6. The Conservative Party's **volte-face** astonished the press even more than most members of the opposition party.

   a. ☐ complete reversal in policy
   b. ☐ covert maneuvering
   c. ☐ final stand on a matter
   d. ☐ hypocritical stance
   e. ☐ reason for taking action

7. She had consumed all of her **quotidian** food ration, and bedtime still was hours away.

   a. ☐ meager
   b. ☐ daily
   c. ☐ normal
   d. ☐ overly generous
   e. ☐ carefully planned

8. **Xenophobes** have no problem in finding others who share their condition.

   a. ☐ persons who have difficulty in making friends
   b. ☐ persons with strong dislike of exotic foods
   c. ☐ persons who mistrust their neighbors
   d. ☐ persons with strong dislike of foreigners
   e. ☐ persons fearful of contracting disease by contact with others

9. Although found guilty of **misprision,** the mayor did not see fit to resign.

   a. ☐ embezzlement of public funds
   b. ☐ bribe-taking by a public official
   c. ☐ neglect or wrongful action by a public official

d. ☐   wrongful use of office to promote one's own financial interests

e. ☐   crime carrying a penalty of imprisonment of more than one year

10. Most of the brothers took their **refection** when the evening bells fell silent.

a. ☐   small meal

b. ☐   act of withdrawal into contemplation

c. ☐   renewal of vows

d. ☐   resumption of normal duties

e. ☐   recitation of evening prayers

◼ *ZINGERS*

A. **yare:**

a. ☐   with weight of container taken into account

b. ☐   maneuverable

c. ☐   considered archaic

d. ☐   partially taxable

e. ☐   unenlightened

B. **kurtosis:**

a. ☐   abnormal backward curvature of the spine

b. ☐   rapid chemical or physical degradation

c. ☐   excessively rapid fermentation of wine or beer

d. ☐   abrupt change in frequency of seismic activity

e. ☐   sharpness of peak of curve of frequency distribution

Test
FORTY

1. Diane found herself enjoying the process of **disbursing** other people's money instead of her own.

   a. ☐ investing

   b. ☐ expending

   c. ☐ protecting

   d. ☐ saving

   e. ☐ accounting for

2. By the time the prom began, every part of the gymnasium walls the students could reach had been thoroughly **festooned.**

   a. ☐ decorated with hanging ornaments

   b. ☐ covered with flowers

   c. ☐ covered with painted slogans

   d. ☐ decorated with tributes to a favorite teacher

   e. ☐ decorated suitably

3. Press time for my first book was only days away, and I had not completed my compilation of **errata.**

   a. ☐ mistakes in thought

   b. ☐ bibliography of disputed sources

   c. ☐ inconsistencies in style of writing

   d. ☐ errors in writing or printing

   e. ☐ glossary of technical terms

4. Years of consistent practice markedly altered his **flaccid** prose style.

   a. ☐ weak and repetitious

   b. ☐ deficient in imagination

   c. ☐ lacking vigor and energy

d. ☐   lacking focus

e. ☐   characterized by wordiness

5. A beautifully executed **caracole** brought his mount into position for the first jump.

a. ☐   half wheel to right or left

b. ☐   complete wheel to right or left

c. ☐   abrupt increase in speed

d. ☐   abrupt decrease in speed

e. ☐   abrupt change from canter to gallop

6. Everyone knew the third reading of the **banns** was scheduled for the following day.

a. ☐   public notice of censure by church officials

b. ☐   public notice of activities forbidden by church authorities

c. ☐   public notice of ouster of members by church authorities

d. ☐   public notice of new regulations instituted by church authorities

e. ☐   public notice in church announcing forthcoming marriage

7. A display of **dipterous** insects at the museum proved surprisingly popular with students.

a. ☐   having two wings

b. ☐   having two principal body segments

c. ☐   having two sets of eyes

d. ☐   having a two-stage excretory process

e. ☐   having a two-stage digestive process

8. The **plangent** tolling of the bell summoned townspeople to their little church.

a. ☐   audible throughout a large area

b. ☐   conveying urgency

c. ☐   muted

d. ☐   of musical quality

e. ☐   loud and mournful

9. We all admired her ability to exploit the intriguing possibilities of the **villanelle.**

a. ☐   type of verse form

b. ☐   type of suburban architecture

c. ☐   type of novel

d. ☐   type of watercolor

e. ☐   type of oil painting

10. Hollywood showed interest in her best-seller, which told of an **incubus** preying on the married women of the town.

a. ☐   self-styled exorcist lacking church authorization for his activities

b. ☐   spirit said to have intercourse with sleeping women

c. ☐   evangelist with wide following

d. ☐   church organist and choirmaster

e. ☐   merchant offering love potions and infertility cures

■   *ZINGERS*

A. **concinnity:**

a. ☐   motivation stemming from sexual desire

b. ☐   decomposition of an object through extended application of low heat

c. ☐   elegance of literary style

d. ☐   complete agreement in goals and plans

e. ☐   harmonious relationship between people with common aims

B. **gadroon:**

a. ☐   military unit assigned dangerous missions

b. ☐   person of mixed racial heritage

c. ☐   man who flits about in society

d. ☐   series of convex curves forming decorative edge

e. ☐   set of symbols said to have magical powers

Test
FORTY-ONE

1. Once the special prosecutor gained the power of subpoena, there was little the senators could do to **extricate** themselves.

a. ☐   free from a difficulty

b. ☐   exonerate

c. ☐   hide crimes successfully

d. ☐   claim innocence for

e. ☐   explain one's actions

2. The unanticipated **hiatus** completely destroyed the close attention our committee had enjoyed until then.

a. ☐   noisy public demonstration

b. ☐   rest period

c. ☐   enthusiastic response of an audience

d. ☐   break in continuity

e. ☐   interruption for questions

3. That I was offended by her **gratuitous** insult goes without saying.

a. ☐   entirely unexpected

b. ☐   carefully rehearsed

c. ☐ ill-timed

d. ☐ uncalled for

e. ☐ showing lack of gratitude

4. It was feared he would **arrogate** powers traditionally held by others.

   a. ☐ quietly ignore

   b. ☐ seize without justification

   c. ☐ refuse to recognize

   d. ☐ share equally in

   e. ☐ subject to challenge

5. A veritable **gerontocracy** emerged that was to survive almost until the end of the second century.

   a. ☐ unrestrained admiration for aged people

   b. ☐ rule by the wisest

   c. ☐ governmental usurpation by the aged

   d. ☐ privileged ruling class

   e. ☐ government by a council of elders

6. **Enuresis** remained a problem for James well beyond adolescence.

   a. ☐ inflammatory condition of the skin

   b. ☐ excessive shyness

   c. ☐ involuntary urination

   d. ☐ general awkwardness

   e. ☐ daydreaming

7. Again, as in several years past, the young girl took first prize for **manege.**

   a. ☐ horsemanship

   b. ☐ table manners

c. ☐   courtesy

d. ☐   attendance

e. ☐   skill in learning foreign languages

8. **Glabrous** skin differentiates the species, making identification fairly easy even for beginners.

a. ☐   scaly

b. ☐   wet to the touch

c. ☐   smooth or bald

d. ☐   ridged

e. ☐   covered with spikes

9. The headmaster is unsurpassed in **objurgation** and finds ample opportunity to practice his skill.

a. ☐   motivation of young pupils

b. ☐   forceful use of well-chosen words

c. ☐   control of expenditures

d. ☐   avoidance of assigned tasks

e. ☐   harsh denunciation

10. We are justified in marveling at **holophrastic** languages.

a. ☐   entirely lacking tenses

b. ☐   expressing entire phrases or groups of ideas in a word

c. ☐   having only two tenses

d. ☐   having words of only one meaning each

e. ☐   unambiguous in expression

■ *ZINGERS*

A. **gnosis:** knowledge of

a. ☐   philosophic methods of reasoning

b. ☐   worldly matters

c. ☐   philosophic theory of signs and symbols

d. ☐   general semantics

e. ☐   spiritual mysteries

B. **palpebral:** of the

a. ☐   lower lip

b. ☐   skin of the scalp

c. ☐   eyelids

d. ☐   sense of touch

e. ☐   sense of taste

Test
FORTY-TWO

1. Who could not have been affected by the **dirge** they played?

a. ☐   song expressing joy

b. ☐   song of celebration

c. ☐   slow mournful song

d. ☐   patriotic marching music

e. ☐   music for drums and horns

2. **Explicit** instructions have been issued to cover situations of that type.

a. ☐   objectively stated

b. ☐   consisting of words and drawings

c. ☐ written from the point of view of the reader

d. ☐ stated in detail

e. ☐ well organized

3. An **inordinate** number of tax returns were lost or destroyed during 1986.

a. ☐ excessive

b. ☐ exceedingly small

c. ☐ within expectations

d. ☐ uncounted

e. ☐ additional

4. Children enjoy playing in a **cul-de-sac.**

a. ☐ drain crossing under a road

b. ☐ large cardboard box

c. ☐ refrigerator no longer put to customary use

d. ☐ a type of farm machine

e. ☐ street closed at one end

5. They built the **hogan** large enough to hold all the family possessions.

a. ☐ Indian dwelling built of logs and mud

b. ☐ horse-drawn wooden skid used by Indians

c. ☐ sturdy Indian chest made of wood

d. ☐ Indian tent made of skins and wooden poles

e. ☐ Indian temporary shelter

6. Gallup found the number of American voters favoring the legislation barely **mensurable.**

a. ☐ capable of being measured

b. ☐ more than a majority

c. ☐   less than a majority

d. ☐   worth mentioning

e. ☐   predictable

7. Deeply imbedded in her major poetry we perceive a belief in **solipsism.**

a. ☐   theory that nothing has value except personal experience

b. ☐   theory that truth can only be judged through actual experience

c. ☐   theory that the self is the only knowable or only existent thing

d. ☐   theory that the actions of others cannot be evaluated correctly without taking account of the intentions behind the actions

e. ☐   theory that logical factual knowledge is the only acceptable basis for human action

8. Whom can we call on to supply the **cerements?**

a. ☐   ceremonial objects

b. ☐   cloth coverings for burial of the dead

c. ☐   types of grain used in animal feed

d. ☐   medicinal preparations mixed with wax and resins

e. ☐   utensils made of clay fired at high temperatures

9. It was when he referred to me as a **Pecksniff** that I first took notice of him.

a. ☐   person given to showing distrust of another by sniffing loudly

b. ☐   person who habitually accuses others of committing unjust acts of which he is himself guilty

c. ☐   skillful liar

   d. ☐   selfish and corrupt person hiding behind a show of benevolence

   e. ☐   person who chooses never to indicate approval for achievements of others

10. On the final day of the meeting, two papers were given on recently observed **benthic** plants.

   a. ☐   supportive of other organisms living nearby

   b. ☐   parasitic

   c. ☐   offering potential benefit for human beings

   d. ☐   primitive

   e. ☐   occurring at the bottom of a body of water

■ *ZINGERS*

A. **mythopoeia:**

   a. ☐   reliance on myths for literary allusion

   b. ☐   inspiration gained from reading myths

   c. ☐   use of mythology for creating characters in a literary work

   d. ☐   construction of myths

   e. ☐   interpretation of myths

B. **aposiopesis:** a rhetorical device characterized by

   a. ☐   coupling of contrasting elements within a sentence to call attention to the contrast

   b. ☐   sudden breaking off of a thought as though unwilling or unable to continue

   c. ☐   intentional repetition of key words or phrases

   d. ☐   intentional omission of sentence elements to achieve desired ambiguity

   e. ☐   juxtaposition of syntactically parallel nouns

Test
FORTY-THREE

1. We anticipate **opportune** introduction of computer software.

 a. ☐ rapid

 b. ☐ simultaneous

 c. ☐ occurring at a favorable time

 d. ☐ accomplished with great skill

 e. ☐ done without regard for competitors

2. Simon's **bilious** cynicism brought him a degree of recognition among men and women he thought of as friends.

 a. ☐ extremely unpleasant

 b. ☐ sharply expressed

 c. ☐ persistent

 d. ☐ occasional

 e. ☐ showing poor judgment

3. Even expensive modern homes seldom include a **scullery.**

 a. ☐ room intended for contemplation and reading

 b. ☐ room in which food is cleaned prior to cooking and where dishes are washed and stored

 c. ☐ room in the back of a house where family members can remove and store outer clothing and shoes

 d. ☐ room in an attic for older children

 e. ☐ nursery

4. In his later years, the minister turned his attention more and more to **secular** problems.

 a. ☐ theological

 b. ☐ occurring rarely

 c. ☐ relating to personal behavior

   d. ☐ widespread

   e. ☐ concerned with worldly affairs

5. The attorney insisted that there was no way that all **aleatory** elements could be anticipated in drafting the contract.

   a. ☐ relating to personal preference

   b. ☐ unpredictable

   c. ☐ existing for a brief period

   d. ☐ relating to conveyance of an estate after death

   e. ☐ foreign

6. Because the time for job interviews is drawing near, I surely must give thought to **titivating** my old wardrobe.

   a. ☐ cleaning

   b. ☐ buying

   c. ☐ filling out

   d. ☐ sprucing up

   e. ☐ discarding

7. The proposed **paradigm** proved even more useful than we originally expected.

   a. ☐ geometric shape

   b. ☐ self-contradictory statement appearing to be true

   c. ☐ model of perfection

   d. ☐ optical configuration

   e. ☐ example or pattern

8. I consider myself a card-carrying **Luddite,** unalterably opposed to modern economic policy.

   a. ☐ advocate of full exploitation of labor-saving machinery

   b. ☐ opponent of introduction of labor-saving machinery

c. ☐ advocate of programs to encourage full employment

d. ☐ advocate of financial aid for the poor

e. ☐ opponent of financial aid for the poor

9. Well-nigh **procrustean** management techniques brought him success early in his career.

a. ☐ implemented without regard for employee satisfaction

b. ☐ allowing no deviation whatsoever

c. ☐ tending to enforce conformity through violent methods

d. ☐ dictatorial

e. ☐ free-wheeling

10. Consultant after consultant commented on the apparent eagerness of most managers to respond even to the **velleities** of the chief executive officer.

a. ☐ slight wishes or inclinations

b. ☐ shows of bad temper

c. ☐ indirectly expressed orders

d. ☐ instances of poor judgment

e. ☐ hasty decisions

■ *ZINGERS*

A. **carpophagous:** feeding on

a. ☐ decaying wood

b. ☐ fungus

c. ☐ fruits

d. ☐ nuts

e. ☐ rotting flesh

B. **pantisocracy:** utopian community in which all

  a. ☐ men play the dominant role

  b. ☐ women play the dominant role

  c. ☐ adult males rule

  d. ☐ adult females rule

  e. ☐ men and women are equal and rule

Test
FORTY-FOUR

1. From Burton's own diaries, we can conclude that he exaggerated without **compunction.**

  a. ☐ evil intent

  b. ☐ consideration of effects on others

  c. ☐ twinge of regret

  d. ☐ hesitation

  e. ☐ knowledge of doing so

2. Barbara once again took advantage of the afternoon sun to **ensconce** herself beside the pool.

  a. ☐ tan

  b. ☐ settle comfortably

  c. ☐ amuse

  d. ☐ subject to careful examination

  e. ☐ indulge in excessive drinking

3. **Cursory** inspection is not expected to reveal faults in that component.

  a. ☐ careful

  b. ☐ visual

c. ☐   regular

d. ☐   surprise

e. ☐   hurried

4. Sounds **emanating** from the building impelled rescuers to continue their efforts.

a. ☐   originating from

b. ☐   continuing to be heard

c. ☐   diminishing in intensity

d. ☐   increasing in intensity

e. ☐   being heard less frequently

5. It was common knowledge that she received close friends in **dishabille.**

a. ☐   a state of partial undress

b. ☐   a state of intoxication

c. ☐   a state of deep despair

d. ☐   a state of emotional detachment

e. ☐   a state of agitation

6. Even now, criminologists cannot identify all the causes of **recidivism.**

a. ☐   periodic increase in crime

b. ☐   periodic reduction in crime

c. ☐   apparent need to return to a place where one has committed crime

d. ☐   tendency to employ the same methods repeatedly in committing crime

e. ☐   tendency toward repetition of criminal behavior

7. Soon enough, Dave's **fatuous** responses to Diane's every remark made her realize that the marriage she contemplated would be a terrible mistake.

    a. ☐ sarcastic

    b. ☐ foolish

    c. ☐ evasive

    d. ☐ angry

    e. ☐ sullen

8. Have you thought about the consequences of your **obduracy?**

    a. ☐ lack of ambition

    b. ☐ irregular personal habits

    c. ☐ intellectual arrogance

    d. ☐ stubbornness

    e. ☐ unwillingness to make decisions

9. The initial response to her **rebarbative** face quickly dissipates once she begins to lecture.

    a. ☐ strikingly beautiful

    b. ☐ plain

    c. ☐ unattractive

    d. ☐ masculine in appearance

    e. ☐ scarred

10. Once the **pandect** is published, scholars will have an opportunity to revise their understanding of the achievements of the dominant society in that period.

    a. ☐ account of everything known at a particular time in history

    b. ☐ complete body of laws of a country

    c. ☐ description of customs of a people

d. ☐   encyclopedic presentation of information

e. ☐   collection of interpretations by scholars representing conflicting points of view

■ *ZINGERS*

A. **carphology:** in delirious patients,

a. ☐   protracted moaning

b. ☐   picking at bedclothes

c. ☐   continual screaming

d. ☐   scratching at one's own skin

e. ☐   continual working of the jaws resembling chewing

B. **tobe:** in some parts of Africa,

a. ☐   an outer garment

b. ☐   a gourd used for drinking

c. ☐   a ceremonial jug

d. ☐   a spear

e. ☐   a priest's mask

Test
FORTY-FIVE

1. Such actions surely will retard the **demise** of the institution.

a. ☐   death

b. ☐   growth in power

c. ☐   reduction in effectiveness

d. ☐   slow decay

e. ☐   gradual increase in effectiveness

2. Governments have been known to find **bicameral** legislatures difficult to manage.

   a. ☐   divided in leadership
   b. ☐   composed of members of two political parties equal or nearly equal in number
   c. ☐   hopelessly divided in political beliefs
   d. ☐   functioning by a two-step process
   e. ☐   having two chambers

3. He could not resist the impulse to **flaunt** his lack of formal education.

   a. ☐   deny
   b. ☐   mention
   c. ☐   parade
   d. ☐   hide
   e. ☐   use as an excuse

4. Don't laugh when you see the expensive **creel** he bought.

   a. ☐   kilt
   b. ☐   deerstalker
   c. ☐   crossbow
   d. ☐   fisherman's wicker basket
   e. ☐   set of garden tools

5. It was clear he alone thought his voice was **mellifluous.**

   a. ☐   outstanding
   b. ☐   sweet sounding
   c. ☐   attractive
   d. ☐   below average in quality
   e. ☐   worthy of consideration

6. Although there was no denying her **élan,** some questioned whether it would endure for long.

    a. ☐ vivacity

    b. ☐ natural talent

    c. ☐ strong self-confidence

    d. ☐ talent for making others feel comfortable

    e. ☐ intellectual strength

7. One thing I found objectionable was the widespread **misanthropy** I detected during my visit.

    a. ☐ distrust of strangers

    b. ☐ air of superiority

    c. ☐ dislike of people in general

    d. ☐ bigotry

    e. ☐ intellectual arrogance

8. I find a **retroussé** nose charming and do not understand why she is considering plastic surgery.

    a. ☐ tiny

    b. ☐ prominent

    c. ☐ wide

    d. ☐ turned up

    e. ☐ curved

9. The latest issue of the magazine offers something less than the expected **pabulum.**

    a. ☐ political argument

    b. ☐ food for thought

    c. ☐ assortment of personal essays

    d. ☐ mixture of poetry and fiction

    e. ☐ advice for parents of infants

10. Much can be learned through careful analysis of his **imago.**

   a. ☐ personality cultivated for display on public occasions
   b. ☐ inner life revealed in one's paintings
   c. ☐ doodling
   d. ☐ early artistic effort
   e. ☐ idealized mental image of a person

■ *ZINGERS*

A. **rugose:**

   a. ☐ wrinkled
   b. ☐ flattened
   c. ☐ anxious
   d. ☐ deprived of nourishment
   e. ☐ rich in fats

B. **cunctation:**

   a. ☐ caution
   b. ☐ delay
   c. ☐ uncertainty
   d. ☐ depravity
   e. ☐ enmity

Test
FORTY-SIX

1. We have decided to withhold **approbation** until it can be shown that all prescribed procedures have been followed.

    a. ☐   approval

    b. ☐   consideration

    c. ☐   disapproval

    d. ☐   final decision

    e. ☐   punishment

2. Anyone **imbued** with a sense of right and wrong will see the jury's decision as a miscarriage of justice.

    a. ☐   reared from birth

    b. ☐   inspired

    c. ☐   possessing

    d. ☐   religiously indoctrinated

    e. ☐   fully educated

3. The mechanism used to **jettison** the booster rocket threatened the safety of the crew.

    a. ☐   release intentionally

    b. ☐   ignite

    c. ☐   lock into place

    d. ☐   provide fuel for

    e. ☐   prepare for ignition

4. The study focused on the effects of **cupidity** rather than on how widespread the trait is in most societies.

    a. ☐   laziness

    b. ☐   inability to read or write any language

c. ☐ greed for financial gain

d. ☐ unwillingness to cooperate

e. ☐ lack of common sense

5. New **genres** vanish so rapidly that even keen observers barely have time to take notice of them before they are gone from the scene.

a. ☐ talents

b. ☐ styles or kinds of art or literature

c. ☐ schools of aesthetics or philosophy

d. ☐ techniques

e. ☐ psychoanalytic theories

6. What surprised all of us was the **animus** obvious in speech after speech at the meeting.

a. ☐ spiteful ill will

b. ☐ good humor

c. ☐ willingness to cooperate

d. ☐ lack of prejudice

e. ☐ liveliness of thought

7. To her profound disgust, most critics agreed the play never rose above **bathos.**

a. ☐ mere sensationalism

b. ☐ self-praise

c. ☐ self-pity

d. ☐ exploitation of interest in sex

e. ☐ quality arousing insincere sadness

8. The artist's female models reflected his taste for figures decidedly inclined to **embonpoint.**

a. ☐   slenderness

b. ☐   fullness of bosom and hips

c. ☐   extreme tallness

d. ☐   excessive plumpness

e. ☐   attractiveness

9. In the next year, scientists from several nations will cooperate in a census of **pelagic** plants and animals.

a. ☐   occurring in tropical climates

b. ☐   occurring in the open sea

c. ☐   occurring on subarctic terrain

d. ☐   occurring at or near the equator

e. ☐   occurring in temperate climates

10. **Saprophagous** beetles fulfill an important function in the web of life.

a. ☐   feeding on dung

b. ☐   feeding on insects

c. ☐   feeding on decaying matter

d. ☐   feeding on other beetles

e. ☐   feeding on spiders

■   *ZINGERS*

A. **nisus:**

a. ☐   denial

b. ☐   repugnance

c. ☐   apathy

d. ☐   hostility

e. ☐   impulse

B. **pirogue:** a type of

a. ☐ potato-filled pastry

b. ☐ canoe

c. ☐ ballet dancer's step

d. ☐ deadly South American fish

e. ☐ deciduous shrub

Test
FORTY-SEVEN

1. From then on, according to his physician, even the pleasures of an occasional **aperitif** were forbidden.

a. ☐ mildly alcoholic drink

b. ☐ mixed alcoholic drink

c. ☐ alcoholic drink taken at bedtime to bring on sleep

d. ☐ alcoholic drink taken as an appetizer

e. ☐ glass of wine or beer taken with meals

2. As had become his habit in the evening, Dr. English sat alone with a bottle of bourbon beside him and drank steadily until he became almost **comatose.**

a. ☐ unaware of one's surroundings

b. ☐ able to face life

c. ☐ free of worry

d. ☐ unnaturally inactive and sleepy

e. ☐ pleasantly intoxicated

3. Olive could not understand how rapidly she had become a **frump.**

   a. ☐   woman who invites attentions of men

   b. ☐   woman whom men avoid

   c. ☐   constantly complaining woman

   d. ☐   woman given to gossiping

   e. ☐   unstylish and old-fashioned woman

4. Even repeated viewing of vivid films showing scenes of modern warfare will not **inure** a soldier to the terror of actual battle.

   a. ☐   accustom by experience

   b. ☐   make acceptable by

   c. ☐   make understandable to

   d. ☐   adequately prepare

   e. ☐   prevent understanding by

5. Michael saw his semester's grades as the **harbinger** of an unending string of failures.

   a. ☐   something that announces what is to come

   b. ☐   means of prevention

   c. ☐   final and most striking example

   d. ☐   sudden turnaround of personal fortunes

   e. ☐   clear first instance

6. Janice was off on her **matutinal** walk when the shocking news came.

   a. ☐   occurring daily

   b. ☐   occurring in the evening

   c. ☐   occurring after meals

   d. ☐   occurring in the morning

   e. ☐   occurring before meals

7. A Beethoven sonata provided the never-failing **anodyne** he sought.

a. ☐   something that brings excitement

b. ☐   something that brings pleasure

c. ☐   something that soothes

d. ☐   something that heightens interest

e. ☐   something that relieves feelings of loneliness

8. Even a **percipient** parent does not always know how to deal with every situation.

a. ☐   remembering one's own youth

b. ☐   sympathetic

c. ☐   marked by caring

d. ☐   highly intelligent

e. ☐   quick to notice

9. The hour for **orisons** had passed, and still there was no sign of Catherine.

a. ☐   silent reflections

b. ☐   prayers

c. ☐   group discussions

d. ☐   conferences with a leader

e. ☐   periods of study

10. Most of the members of the committee knew immediately they were dealing with a **rara avis.**

a. ☐   immature person

b. ☐   person of many talents

c. ☐   person or thing rarely encountered

d. ☐   person of outstanding but undeveloped ability

e. ☐   person of unusual sensitivity to the feelings of others

■ *ZINGERS*

A. **paronomasia:**

a. ☐ coining of product names

b. ☐ coining of nicknames

c. ☐ serial placement of sentence elements without indicating subordination or coordination

d. ☐ play on words

e. ☐ practice of levitation and telepathy

B. **schadenfreude:**

a. ☐ malicious enjoyment of other people's troubles

b. ☐ obsessive preoccupation with death

c. ☐ abrupt alternating in mood between elation and depression

d. ☐ combination of sadistic and masochistic behavior in one person

e. ☐ morbid avoidance of unpleasantness in any form

Test
FORTY-EIGHT

1. One **urchin** even came up to me to ask whether I needed help with my packages.

a. ☐ errand boy

b. ☐ young beggar

c. ☐ mischievous youngster

d. ☐ helpful youngster

e. ☐ lost youngster

2. Many times during recent years, he has suffered bouts of **vertigo** that totally incapacitated him.

   a. ☐   depression

   b. ☐   unnatural hunger or thirst

   c. ☐   muscular weakness

   d. ☐   dizziness

   e. ☐   unnatural fear of heights

3. After a week on the job, she had the **temerity** to request a day off.

   a. ☐   bad luck

   b. ☐   impulse

   c. ☐   good sense

   d. ☐   courage

   e. ☐   foolish boldness

4. During that decade ultimate power was in the hands of a **troika.**

   a. ☐   self-appointed revolutionary council

   b. ☐   ruling body of three

   c. ☐   secret council

   d. ☐   person of near-dictatorial power

   e. ☐   ruling body of unelected officials

5. Sitting quietly on a park bench in the sun, he took **vicarious** pleasure from observing young couples as they strolled hand in hand.

   a. ☐   experienced through activity of others

   b. ☐   unnatural or unwholesome

   c. ☐   much-needed

   d. ☐   distorted

   e. ☐   affording much satisfaction

6. For hours I watched Emily's **supine** body, wondering whether I ever again would see her on her feet.

   a. ☐ lying face upward

   b. ☐ entirely motionless

   c. ☐ slender and attractive

   d. ☐ slowly dying

   e. ☐ severely wounded

7. Immediate action will surely **roil** the executive committee.

   a. ☐ encourage

   b. ☐ satisfy

   c. ☐ annoy

   d. ☐ hamper

   e. ☐ delight

8. Scholars were pleased when church officials announced that the **reliquary** would be made available for study.

   a. ☐ ancient burial site

   b. ☐ ancient scroll

   c. ☐ collection of objects used in worship

   d. ☐ bones of religious martyrs

   e. ☐ container for religious relics

9. Late in the afternoon, the research team came upon yet another **xenolith.**

   a. ☐ early stone drawing

   b. ☐ example of an artist's early work

   c. ☐ work of art unlike the typical art of a period

   d. ☐ rock fragment within rock of a different type

   e. ☐ upright inscribed stone pillar

155

10. **Williwaws** come up without warning to populations along mountainous coasts.

   a. ☐ sudden sharp drops in barometric pressure and temperature

   b. ☐ sudden cold windstorms

   c. ☐ storms of mixed hail and rain

   d. ☐ localized storms with whirling winds

   e. ☐ sudden sharp rises in barometric pressure and temperature

■   *ZINGERS*

A. **zeugma:**

   a. ☐ pyramidal tower in ancient Mesopotamia with a temple on top

   b. ☐ use of a verb or adjective with two nouns even though the verb or adjective is strictly applicable only to one

   c. ☐ rhetorical device in which emphasis is achieved through deliberate repetition of identical words or phrases

   d. ☐ situation in which a chess player is limited to disadvantageous moves

   e. ☐ representation of idioms in one language in appropriate idioms of a different language

B. **refulgence:**

   a. ☐ unrestrained expression of emotions

   b. ☐ resistance to control or discipline

   c. ☐ excessive praise or adulation

   d. ☐ feeling of extreme repugnance

   e. ☐ shining and gloriously bright state

Test
FORTY-NINE

1. They labeled **bourgeois** anyone whose tastes differed from their own.

   a. ☐   member of the working class

   b. ☐   person lacking ideas worth considering

   c. ☐   person of unrefined tastes

   d. ☐   person with conventional middle-class ideas

   e. ☐   person lacking adequate knowledge of art and literature

2. Irene remained an **habitué** of the establishment long after her friends had given it up.

   a. ☐   strong admirer

   b. ☐   welcome guest

   c. ☐   faithful employee

   d. ☐   principal supporter

   e. ☐   regular visitor

3. I believe Jeff wonders why no one pays much attention to his **idiosyncrasies** anymore.

   a. ☐   selfish attitudes

   b. ☐   foolish claims or ideas

   c. ☐   characteristics peculiar to a person

   d. ☐   statements intended to impress others

   e. ☐   statements showing brilliance

4. Successful copywriters always manage to come up with a **fillip** that sets their work apart.

   a. ☐   something that excites interest

   b. ☐   clever phrase that sticks in one's memory

   c. ☐   compelling theme

157

d. ☐ brilliant image

e. ☐ new way of saying something

5. The couple that came to see our house obviously failed to appreciate its **bucolic** charm.

    a. ☐ compact in arrangement

    b. ☐ characteristic of country life

    c. ☐ old-fashioned

    d. ☐ modern in furnishings

    e. ☐ suitable for family life

6. Physicians quickly ruled out the possibility of an **occluded** blood vessel and looked elsewhere for the underlying cause of Pam's condition.

    a. ☐ weakened

    b. ☐ twisted

    c. ☐ thinned

    d. ☐ torn

    e. ☐ obstructed

7. Much to Michael's surprise, his professional competence and **languid** manner attracted clients to his law practice.

    a. ☐ showing understanding

    b. ☐ sharp and precise

    c. ☐ lacking vigor

    d. ☐ positive and unswerving

    e. ☐ smooth

8. By then he was even willing to attempt dishes cooked in **papillote.**

    a. ☐ thin flaky pastry

    b. ☐ greased paper wrapper

c. ☐ chicken stock

d. ☐ Burgundy wine

e. ☐ thick pastry crust

9. When the bottle of **retsina** arrived at the table, my heart sank.

a. ☐ resin-flavored Greek wine

b. ☐ sweet Alsatian wine

c. ☐ fortified Mediterranean wine

d. ☐ liqueur flavored with aniseed

e. ☐ Turkish wine punch

10. As often was the case, her **perspicuous** remarks were discussed for days after the meeting.

a. ☐ clearly expressed

b. ☐ entirely inappropriate

c. ☐ lacking in judgment or insight

d. ☐ highly inflammatory

e. ☐ intentionally insulting

▚ ZINGERS

A. **diapason:**

a. ☐ almost transparent dress material

b. ☐ substance inducing perspiration

c. ☐ melody that swells grandly

d. ☐ spasmodic expansion of the heart

e. ☐ constitutional predisposition to disease

B. **poetaster:**

a. ☐ poet possessing high powers of imagination

b. ☐ obsequious flatterer of poets

c. ☐   inferior poet

d. ☐   unperceptive critic of poetry

e. ☐   poetry anthologist

Test
FIFTY

1. New weapon systems are designed to **wreak** punishment on enemy forces before those forces mobilize.

a. ☐   threaten

b. ☐   maximize

c. ☐   inflict

d. ☐   reduce

e. ☐   increase

2. In our country, a person threatened with imminent death should be warned about dying **intestate.**

a. ☐   not having appointed a legal guardian for one's children

b. ☐   not having designated an attorney to protect one's heirs

c. ☐   not having designated an executor of one's will

d. ☐   not having made a will

e. ☐   not having protected the rights of one's spouse

3. The town erected a memorial in **veneration** of the fallen president.

a. ☐   perpetuation of the memory of someone

b. ☐   expression of a feeling of great respect

c. ☐   repayment of a debt for favors shown

d. ☐   demonstration of regard for the family of a dead person

e. ☐   recognition of someone's achievements

4. From then on, no one challenged Frank's reputation as a first-class **mountebank.**

    a. ☐ financial manipulator

    b. ☐ teller of tall tales

    c. ☐ ladies' man

    d. ☐ card sharp

    e. ☐ swindler

5. The dean of students described our dormitory as having all the charm of a **rookery.**

    a. ☐ breeding place of certain birds or mammals

    b. ☐ gambling casino

    c. ☐ garbage dump

    d. ☐ national political convention

    e. ☐ meeting of political leaders

6. After an hour with the unfinished dissertation, Elaine knew her **torpid** mind would produce little that day.

    a. ☐ troubled

    b. ☐ sluggish

    c. ☐ lacking necessary inspiration

    d. ☐ occupied with unrelated matters

    e. ☐ normally brilliant

7. Marilyn was perceived more as a Venus than an **undine.**

    a. ☐ vestal virgin

    b. ☐ innocent child

    c. ☐ water nymph

    d. ☐ model of female behavior

    e. ☐ mysterious creature of the forest

8. At about that time, the first accurate **goniometer** made its appearance.

a. ☐ instrument for measuring angles
b. ☐ instrument for measuring parts of the body
c. ☐ surveyor's instrument for measuring distances
d. ☐ instrument for computing volumes
e. ☐ instrument for determining the dip of the earth's magnetic force

9. Success of the mission hinged on securing the services of at least three experienced **dragomans.**

a. ☐ senior diplomats
b. ☐ local officials
c. ☐ supervisors of unskilled laborers
d. ☐ interpreters or guides
e. ☐ equipment and supply carriers

10. From the start, Klee avoided the **fulgent** patterns of color that marked the work of most of his contemporaries.

a. ☐ contrasting
b. ☐ thickly applied
c. ☐ merging one into another
d. ☐ complementary
e. ☐ dazzling

■ *ZINGERS*

A. **videlicet:**

a. ☐ on the other hand
b. ☐ in addition
c. ☐ for example

d. ☐ by contrast

e. ☐ namely

B. **ziggurat:** in ancient Mesopotamia, a

a. ☐ multi-storied pyramidal tower surmounted by a temple

b. ☐ sacred structure entered only by members of the clergy

c. ☐ watering place for nomadic tribesmen and their herds

d. ☐ apartment in a palace for the residence of women

e. ☐ room in a palace for entertaining male visitors

Test
FIFTY-ONE

1. From the time the grandchildren arrived, we were confronted with unending **bedlam.**

a. ☐ family disputes

b. ☐ family pleasures

c. ☐ prolonged bouts of eating and drinking

d. ☐ scene of uproar

e. ☐ petty arguments

2. As hard as we tried we were not able to **efface** the signs of the intrusion.

a. ☐ forget

b. ☐ change

c. ☐ recall

d. ☐ obliterate

e. ☐ lighten

3. Everyone agreed that Ron was guilty of nothing more than a **faux pas.**

    a. ☐ misdemeanor

    b. ☐ major error of judgment

    c. ☐ embarrassing blunder

    d. ☐ petty crime

    e. ☐ minor act of snobbery

4. From the way the judge treats us, you would think we were nothing more than **hoi polloi.**

    a. ☐ unskilled workmen

    b. ☐ rabble

    c. ☐ beginners

    d. ☐ personal servants

    e. ☐ slaves

5. The statement meant a great deal to us because Herbert was **chary** with his praise.

    a. ☐ generous

    b. ☐ eloquent

    c. ☐ sincere

    d. ☐ fair

    e. ☐ sparing

6. You can count on Norma to lay out all the **accoutrements** imaginable.

    a. ☐ articles of equipment

    b. ☐ vital facts in a discussion

    c. ☐ conflicting points of view

    d. ☐ items of food for a complete meal

    e. ☐ reasons for voting against a proposed bill

7. Once we joined the department, we knew why Mr. Thomas was known as an **officious** manager.

   a. ☐ careful about matters small and large

   b. ☐ productive

   c. ☐ insulting

   d. ☐ very ambitious

   e. ☐ meddlesome

8. The longer we listened to the **philippic,** the more obvious it became that the old politician had lost his touch.

   a. ☐ explanation

   b. ☐ tribute

   c. ☐ tirade

   d. ☐ appeal for support

   e. ☐ partisan argument

9. It is difficult to find artisans capable of fabricating a **felucca** worthy of the name.

   a. ☐ man's flexible cane made of the stem of a slender palm

   b. ☐ small Mediterranean coasting vessel with oars or sails

   c. ☐ Greek oil lamp with a glassy finish

   d. ☐ villa in the Roman style

   e. ☐ tobacco pipe made of carved meerschaum

10. Countless writers marvel at Baker's **limpid** prose style.

   a. ☐ inventive

   b. ☐ rich in metaphor

   c. ☐ clear

   d. ☐ elegant

   e. ☐ persuasive

■   *ZINGERS*

A. **polder:**

a. ☐   ghost or spirit said to manifest its presence by making noises

b. ☐   transition region between river and sea into which the river empties

c. ☐   massive structure acting as breakwater or pier

d. ☐   low-lying land reclaimed from the sea or river

e. ☐   small insect-eating mammal living chiefly underground

B. **pavid:**

a. ☐   serene

b. ☐   timid

c. ☐   intense

d. ☐   witless

e. ☐   broad

Test
FIFTY-TWO

1. Not surprisingly, their **colloquy** went on all day and far into the night.

a. ☐   open disagreement

b. ☐   conversation

c. ☐   display of antagonism

d. ☐   period of cooperation

e. ☐   refusal to talk

2. Almost as a matter of principle, David never seems **amenable** to arguments advanced by others.

a. ☐   willing to yield

b. ☐   unwilling to agree

c. ☐   openly hostile

d. ☐   expressing fear

e. ☐   willing to compromise

3. No one could understand why Meg looked so **crestfallen** while the honors were being announced.

a. ☐   highly elated

b. ☐   uninterested

c. ☐   sure of success

d. ☐   disappointed at failure

e. ☐   apparently unconcerned

4. Investigators determined that the **bisque** contained the salmonella that felled so many of the diners.

a. ☐   thick cream soup

b. ☐   shellfish

c. ☐   iced dessert

d. ☐   canned fish

e. ☐   pastry-covered liver pâté

5. The entire cast was present to observe completion of the **gibbet.**

a. ☐   stage scenery

b. ☐   back wall of a stage set

c. ☐   large cage for animals

d. ☐   structure for mounting overhead lights

e. ☐   gallows

6. After trying for months, the rebel forces failed to **interdict** supplies of ammunition and food.

    a. ☐   maintain a steady flow

    b. ☐   control distribution

    c. ☐   prohibit to others

    d. ☐   share within a group

    e. ☐   increase

7. For reasons no one can explain, the traditional **nexus** between hard work and eventual success no longer seems to obtain.

    a. ☐   period of time

    b. ☐   delay

    c. ☐   ethical framework

    d. ☐   anticipated reward

    e. ☐   link

8. With your indulgence, I now call attention to the **penultimate** paragraph.

    a. ☐   next to last

    b. ☐   introductory

    c. ☐   concluding

    d. ☐   third

    e. ☐   middle

9. **Rubiginous** birds pause during migration to seek food in farmers' fields.

    a. ☐   feeding on crops

    b. ☐   rust-colored

    c. ☐   feeding on rotting flesh

    d. ☐ .   migrating early

    e. ☐   traveling in large flocks

10. In her research Emily determined that there was a strong relation between food supply and **pelage.**

 a. ☐ hunting behavior of a mammal

 b. ☐ bone structure of a mammal

 c. ☐ fur, hair, wool of a mammal

 d. ☐ skeletal development of a mammal

 e. ☐ digestive system of a mammal

 ■ *ZINGERS*

A. **proem:**

 a. ☐ assertion

 b. ☐ preamble

 c. ☐ response

 d. ☐ allegation

 e. ☐ impassioned demand

B. **regisseur:**

 a. ☐ chief designer of women's clothing

 b. ☐ publicity director

 c. ☐ acting head of an organization

 d. ☐ registrar of trademarks or copyrights

 e. ☐ director or producer of a film or stage production

SUPERWORDPOWER

Test
FIFTY-THREE

1. I do not enjoy finding myself in a **quandary** about whether to roll over my pension money.

   a. □   state of uncertainty

   b. □   embarrassing situation

   c. □   fearful state

   d. □   state of complete ignorance

   e. □   condition of complete reliance on the judgment of advisers

2. The schedule calls for the fourth day's meeting to be a **plenary** session.

   a. □   concluding

   b. □   attended only by officers

   c. □   attended by all members

   d. □   intended for election of new slate of officers

   e. □   largely ceremonial

3. I shall never forget my first day of travel in the Midlands, when I saw my first **gazebo.**

   a. □   type of antelope, noted for graceful movements

   b. □   cottage with a thatched roof

   c. □   structure, such as a summerhouse, built on a site offering an enjoyable view

   d. □   type of ancient Celtic church

   e. □   small pond situated deep in a woods

4. Those who opposed Janet's position on the matter said her objections to the plan were **picayune.**

    a. ☐ based on incomplete information

    b. ☐ logical but biased

    c. ☐ consistently overstated

    d. ☐ designed to obstruct

    e. ☐ petty

5. Some experts predict that **potable** water will soon become a scarce commodity.

    a. ☐ plentiful for use in industrial cooling applications

    b. ☐ drinkable

    c. ☐ easily accessible

    d. ☐ plentiful for use in irrigation

    e. ☐ easily transportable

6. One might expect that much of the dog food canned and sold in our country is **offal.**

    a. ☐ organs of a butchered animal

    b. ☐ nutritious meats ordinarily eaten by humans in other countries

    c. ☐ parts of a butchered animal offering bulk but little else

    d. ☐ parts cut off as waste in butchering an animal

    e. ☐ grains nutritious for humans and animals

7. When Leonard detected a **rale,** he called his patient's family to the bedside.

    a. ☐ abnormal rattling sound accompanying breathing

    b. ☐ sudden drop in body temperature

    c. ☐ marked decline in vital signs

    d. ☐ shallowness of respiration

    e. ☐ sudden rise in body temperature

8. Mencken was known to refer to himself as a **curmudgeon.**

a. ☐ person interested always in getting to the bottom of a matter

b. ☐ bad-tempered old man

c. ☐ person passionately devoted to the truth

d. ☐ person of narrow interests

e. ☐ person of partisan views and interests

9. Astronomers have announced that the moon will be in **perigee** on the sixteenth of next month.

a. ☐ point in orbit farthest from Earth

b. ☐ point in orbit midway between farthest and nearest distances from Earth

c. ☐ point in orbit nearly in straight line between Earth and sun

d. ☐ point in orbit nearest Earth

e. ☐ point in orbit behind Earth, forming nearly a straight line from moon to Earth to sun

10. Although many of our friends feel otherwise, I truly envy his **perseveration.**

a. ☐ ability to comment wisely or clearly

b. ☐ aimless discussion of any topic under consideration

c. ☐ continuation of an activity for an excessively long time

d. ☐ ability to make jokes about serious topics

e. ☐ persistence in reaching for the truth, no matter how distasteful

■ *ZINGERS*

A. **busby:**

a. ☐ dance scene in Hollywood musical film

b. ☐ thick-soled shoe worn by ancient Roman actors

c. ☐ large Old World running bird

d. ☐ tall fur cap worn by British guardsmen

e. ☐ small rural settlement in India

B. **praxis:**

a. ☐ practice, as distinguished from theory

b. ☐ traditional method of prediction

c. ☐ projection based on statistical techniques

d. ☐ seat-of-the-pants estimation

e. ☐ action taken before thorough analysis

Test
FIFTY-FOUR

1. Most people thought the sale of arms to Iran was more than **reprehensible.**

a. ☐ deserving of public distrust

b. ☐ unforgivable

c. ☐ worthy of close examination

d. ☐ praiseworthy

e. ☐ deserving rebuke

2. Successful management of any business, large or small, requires a **whit** of common sense.

a. ☐ average amount

b. ☐ great deal

173

   c. ☐   least possible amount

   d. ☐   small amount

   e. ☐   extraordinary amount

3. By then, according to Cassatt's biographer, her talent had reached its **zenith.**

   a. ☐   lowest point

   b. ☐   highest point

   c. ☐   beginning of full development

   d. ☐   period of first critical recognition

   e. ☐   time of first public acclaim

4. Household objects made in the Bauhaus style remind us of the shortcomings of other **utilitarian** designs.

   a. ☐   meant to be useful rather than decorative

   b. ☐   meant to be decorative

   c. ☐   all-purpose

   d. ☐   single-purpose

   e. ☐   inexpensive

5. For a time that summer, the future president of the country worked as a **roustabout.**

   a. ☐   traveling mender of household utensils

   b. ☐   unskilled worker in oil fields

   c. ☐   stagehand in a traveling show

   d. ☐   cowboy

   e. ☐   circus clown

6. Cultivation of **viniferous** varieties of grapes has increased markedly in recent years.

   a. ☐   grown for the production of wine

   b. ☐   containing a heavy concentration of pulp

c. ☐ containing a great deal of liquid

d. ☐ of excellent flavor

e. ☐ mildly acidic

7. The times call for an authentic **thaumaturge** to solve the world's economic and social ills.

a. ☐ social planner

b. ☐ management expert

c. ☐ inspiring leader

d. ☐ worker of miracles

e. ☐ charismatic religious figure

8. My **quondam** friend saw fit to denounce me before a full meeting of the city council.

a. ☐ two-faced

b. ☐ so-called

c. ☐ apparently trustworthy

d. ☐ former

e. ☐ close

9. His habitual use of **litotes** was a source of annoyance for many of us.

a. ☐ deliberate exaggeration for rhetorical effect

b. ☐ extended argument intended to wear down an opponent's patience

c. ☐ excessively flowery language intended to impress

d. ☐ use of metaphor to make a point indirectly

e. ☐ understatement by expressing an affirmative as the negative of its contrary

10. Who will be there to welcome her as a **revenant?**

  a. ☐ person who has regained faith in God

  b. ☐ person returned from the dead

  c. ☐ person who has experienced religious rebirth

  d. ☐ person who has resumed loyalty to a cause

  e. ☐ person cured of disease thought to be fatal

■ *ZINGERS*

A. **xebec:**

  a. ☐ medieval musical string instrument

  b. ☐ small three-masted Mediterranean vessel

  c. ☐ children's biscuit

  d. ☐ puzzle combining words and pictures

  e. ☐ surgical instrument used for scraping bones

B. **paresthesia:**

  a. ☐ insertion of unrelated matters into a discussion in order to alter its course

  b. ☐ reduction of pain in a small area of the body by application of a mild anesthetic

  c. ☐ abnormal sensation of itching, tingling, and creeping on the skin

  d. ☐ slight or partial temporary paralysis in a limb

  e. ☐ condition marked by occasional bouts of memory loss

Test
FIFTY-FIVE

1. Most Americans consider certain rights to be **inalienable.**

    a. ☐ not able to be taken away

    b. ☐ inappropriate for those who are not citizens

    c. ☐ earned by a person or group

    d. ☐ worthy of enforcement

    e. ☐ not clearly identifiable

2. Who would have believed Bill would turn into a **crotchety** old man so soon after retirement?

    a. ☐ full of aches and pains

    b. ☐ harmless

    c. ☐ lacking interest in anything

    d. ☐ given to grouchiness

    e. ☐ uninteresting

3. After performances I found it intriguing to observe many of the dancers **lumbering** toward their dressing rooms.

    a. ☐ trotting

    b. ☐ walking in a graceful manner

    c. ☐ moving slowly

    d. ☐ walking eagerly

    e. ☐ moving in a heavy, clumsy way

4. There is little doubt in my mind that the film will not be shown in the **hinterlands.**

    a. ☐ regions settled by farmers who originated in northern Europe

    b. ☐ regions populated largely by evangelical Christians

    c. ☐ regions not served by modern modes of transportation

d. ☐   regions inhabited largely by people of low income

e. ☐   regions remote from cities

5. During the course of the year I was unable to learn much about the man you described as a **fakir.**

a. ☐   Muslim or Hindu faith healer

b. ☐   Hindu juggler who performs in the streets and solicits funds

c. ☐   Muslim or Hindu beggar regarded as a holy man

d. ☐   Hindu snake charmer

e. ☐   Muslim street magician

6. Health officials have collected data that indicate the disease is no longer **endemic** anywhere in Asia.

a. ☐   commonly found in a particular region

b. ☐   rarely found

c. ☐   extremely threatening to life

d. ☐   suddenly affecting many people in a region

e. ☐   subject to control by improvement in sanitation

7. At first the physician prescribed a **demulcent** to see whether the discomfort would disappear.

a. ☐   medicine that eases pain in the stomach

b. ☐   medicine that soothes an irritated membrane

c. ☐   medicine that reduces anxiety

d. ☐   medicine that improves breathing by opening clogged respiratory passages

e. ☐   harmless substance given as though it were medicine in order to humor a patient

8. Novelists still turn occasionally to the **epistolary** form.

  a. ☐ in the form of a diary

  b. ☐ using the technique of flashbacks

  c. ☐ represented as historically accurate

  d. ☐ consisting of letters

  e. ☐ taking the reader into the confidence of the principal character

9. We spent an extraordinary evening playing something called **bezique.**

  a. ☐ game played by two teams trying to guess each other's thoughts

  b. ☐ game testing knowledge of recent history

  c. ☐ game resembling pinochle played with sixty-four cards

  d. ☐ game resembling strip poker

  e. ☐ game played by two teams trying to guess identities of players from clever character descriptions supplied by other players

10. Many people in the ghetto firmly believed in the story of the **dybbuk.**

  a. ☐ legendary figure who refused to betray his people to an enemy

  b. ☐ evil spirit said to enter the body of a living person

  c. ☐ artificial human being endowed with life

  d. ☐ legendary protector of the tomb of a messiah

  e. ☐ spirit that restores life to the dead upon the appearance of a messiah

■ *ZINGERS*

A. **pimpernel:**

a. ☐ wild plant with small scarlet, purple, or white flowers
b. ☐ brilliantly colored silken scarf
c. ☐ soldier of fortune active as a spy for his own country
d. ☐ mounted courier serving his country's forces
e. ☐ courtier expert in dueling with swords

B. **wight:**

a. ☐ loop in a rope
b. ☐ means of accomplishing some work
c. ☐ small animal
d. ☐ human being
e. ☐ destiny

Test
FIFTY-SIX

1. Even though we were given just a few sketches to work from, we were able to construct an acceptable **kiosk** in the allotted time.

a. ☐ underground shelter
b. ☐ shallow tank to hold plants growing in nutrient solutions rather than in soil
c. ☐ light structure for sale of newspapers, food, or the like
d. ☐ feeding trough for farm animals
e. ☐ rack for holding magazines and books

2. The agricultural agent made a serious error when she informed us that the site was rich in **loam.**

   a. ☐ organic material providing plant nutrients

   b. ☐ mineral deposits indicative of the presence of petroleum

   c. ☐ material deposited as a result of volcanic activity

   d. ☐ soil capable of holding water and therefore suitable for making ponds

   e. ☐ easily crumbled soil of clay, silt, and sand

3. There is no doubt that my mother appeared **distraught** during the reading of the will.

   a. ☐ unconcerned

   b. ☐ unable to concentrate

   c. ☐ deeply interested

   d. ☐ greatly upset

   e. ☐ completely at ease

4. As part of the preparation for fermentation, we knew we had to **macerate** the malt.

   a. ☐ soften by steeping in a liquid

   b. ☐ grind to reduce size of grains

   c. ☐ grind to separate into usable and unusable parts

   d. ☐ treat to improve flavor or other properties

   e. ☐ treat to halt germination

5. We marveled at the beauty of the old **minarets** we saw during our months in the Middle East.

   a. ☐ detailed carvings found in mosques

   b. ☐ slender towers attached to mosques with balconies from which the faithful are called to prayer

   c. ☐ ornately patterned prayer rugs

    d. ☐   decorative mosaics of religious messages and symbols

    e. ☐   groups of small dwellings arranged about a central square in a town or village

6. Our experiments focused originally on developing more detailed understanding of adolescent **cognition.**

    a. ☐   group behavior

    b. ☐   competitive behavior

    c. ☐   characteristic pattern of responses to irritation or urging

    d. ☐   act or process of perceiving or knowing

    e. ☐   abnormal pattern of excessive self-criticism

7. One of the reasons for making the expedition was to photograph the **dingo** in its natural habitat.

    a. ☐   tree-climbing marsupial

    b. ☐   Australian wild dog

    c. ☐   marsupial with tail adapted for seizing and grasping

    d. ☐   South American animal with protective covering of bony plates

    e. ☐   large venomous lizard of southwestern United States

8. No means had been provided for disposing of the **ordure** seen everywhere in the concentration camps.

    a. ☐   pile of corpses

    b. ☐   organized accumulation of clothing and other personal possessions

    c. ☐   excrement

    d. ☐   type of flesh-eating beetle

    e. ☐   unsanitary condition causing disease in humans

9. Before further design work on the microchip could be undertaken, an effective **algorithm** had to be developed.

   a. ☐ plan for manufacture

   b. ☐ specialized computer language

   c. ☐ laboratory analytic procedure

   d. ☐ method used in large-scale photographic etching

   e. ☐ process or rule for calculating

10. How many times have we heard a musician described as Beethoven **redivivus?**

   a. ☐ surpassed

   b. ☐ openly imitated

   c. ☐ come back to life

   d. ☐ clearly profaned

   e. ☐ reconsidered

■   *ZINGERS*

A. **pilule:**

   a. ☐ small pill

   b. ☐ nub of fabric left over after cutting

   c. ☐ hairy growth on skin

   d. ☐ ancient Roman dagger

   e. ☐ shallow rectangular architectural decoration

B. **griffin:** in India, a

   a. ☐ tax collector empowered to retain a specified portion of funds collected

   b. ☐ member of privileged caste

   c. ☐ peasant who owns a small amount of land

   d. ☐ newcomer, especially a European

   e. ☐ magistrate in a minor provincial court

Test
FIFTY-SEVEN

1. As expected, he delivered a talk **replete** with clichés and tired anecdotes.

    a. ☐   abundantly supplied

    b. ☐   sprinkled

    c. ☐   badly decorated

    d. ☐   obscured

    e. ☐   combined

2. Once we knew she had come through **unscathed,** our spirits revived.

    a. ☐   unchallenged by other competitors

    b. ☐   unindicted by a grand jury

    c. ☐   without suffering injury

    d. ☐   unchanged in belief

    e. ☐   unwilling to compromise a position

3. As an expert **numismatist** she will give testimony expected to carry great weight with the jury.

    a. ☐   specialist in coins or related objects

    b. ☐   student of Arabic grammar

    c. ☐   historian specializing in recent papal diplomacy

    d. ☐   interpreter of the effects of numbers, particularly date of birth, on the life of a person

    e. ☐   person who claims to communicate with the dead

4. As long as you remain **pervious** to reason, I believe the faculty committee will stand firm in its attitude.

    a. ☐   resistant

    b. ☐   able

c. ☐ constant in devotion

d. ☐ accessible

e. ☐ logical in response

5. It was not long before Charlene realized she had found her **métier.**

a. ☐ position in society

b. ☐ means of survival

c. ☐ means of artistic expression

d. ☐ route to independence

e. ☐ trade or profession

6. Ward's **insouciance** has certainly done little for his career as a bureaucrat.

a. ☐ deviousness

b. ☐ insulting manner

c. ☐ laziness in regard to performing work

d. ☐ lack of concern

e. ☐ unsophistication

7. As we watched, we could not fail to be impressed by his **viridity.**

a. ☐ complete competence

b. ☐ naive innocence

c. ☐ excellence of judgment

d. ☐ clarity of understanding

e. ☐ manliness

8. Once the appeal to divine **puissance** proved fruitless, the church declared bankruptcy.

a. ☐ mercy

b. ☐ intervention

c. ☐   great strength or power

d. ☐   sense of righteousness

e. ☐   sympathy and understanding

9. No one liked Richard's **acerbity,** but there was not much we could do about it.

a. ☐   habit of answering questions by posing additional questions

b. ☐   combativeness

c. ☐   domineering attitude

d. ☐   evasiveness

e. ☐   sharpness of manner

10. As one might expect, almost every sentence in the letter contains at least one **trope.**

a. ☐   reference to classical mythology

b. ☐   word used in other than its literal sense

c. ☐   carefully phrased threat

d. ☐   clever distortion of fact

e. ☐   phrase with two meanings, one indecent

■   *ZINGERS*

A. **gravamen:**

a. ☐   argument that succeeds in silencing critics

b. ☐   first three months of human pregnancy

c. ☐   formal response to claim of mistreatment by church officials

d. ☐   essence of an accusation

e. ☐   humane response to a call for assistance

B. **organon:**

a. ☐   postulated unit of energy derived from primal material

b. ☐   idealized image

c. ☐   any specialized structure within a cell

d. ☐   thin stiff transparent fabric of silk or synthetic fiber

e. ☐   means of reasoning

Test
FIFTY-EIGHT

1. Sam could never be called an **indolent** worker by anyone who knew his work habits.

a. ☐   lazy

b. ☐   eager

c. ☐   cooperative

d. ☐   productive

e. ☐   unproductive

2. Mention of Broadway **conjures** up images of bright lights and stunning showgirls.

a. ☐   creates in order to mislead

b. ☐   heightens perception

c. ☐   produces in the mind

d. ☐   creates in order to attract

e. ☐   recalls

3. The rich **patois** once heard in parts of Rhode Island is fast disappearing.

a. ☐   specialized language used by members of a trade

b. ☐   dialect of ordinary people in a region

c. □ broad humor

d. □ specialized language intended to confuse outsiders

e. □ accent heard in a region

4. Before starting work on the project, Ellen estimated the amount of **crewel** she would need.

a. □ library paste

b. □ filler material for wood sculpture

c. □ oak blocking for staircases

d. □ potter's clay

e. □ worsted yarn for embroidery

5. In the opinion of the project manager, Chris now can cope with any foreseeable **exigency.**

a. □ major threat to safety

b. □ problem requiring specialized knowledge

c. □ shortage of funds

d. □ situation demanding prompt action

e. □ breakdown in supply of essential equipment

6. Our director believes Michelle's **fey** look makes her just right for the part.

a. □ showing effects of a lifetime of dissipation

b. □ knowing too much of the ways of the world

c. □ having a strange otherworldly charm

d. □ showing justifiable distrust

e. □ showing childlike innocence

7. Critics frequently remark on her **lapidary** prose style.

a. □ crystal clear

b. □ dignified and concise

c. □ lacking clarity

d. ☐   overly grand

e. ☐   difficult

8. **Otiose** reports of presidential commissions were the rule rather than the exception.

a. ☐   serving no practical purpose

b. ☐   filled with self-praise

c. ☐   vague in expression

d. ☐   grand in expression

e. ☐   lacking specific recommendations

9. The **screes** on that side of Annapurna test the agility of even the best climbers.

a. ☐   sharp drops in terrain ordinarily hidden from view

b. ☐   sheer cliffs difficult to climb

c. ☐   slippery mosses able to grow in extremely cold climates

d. ☐   accumulations of rocky debris on steep mountain slopes

e. ☐   masses of soft snow covered with thin crusts of ice

10. Our regular **sederunt** had lost the fellowship that once infused it.

a. ☐   committee organized to manage annual celebrations

b. ☐   executive group managing day-to-day operations

c. ☐   entertainment committee

d. ☐   loosely organized group of colleagues meeting to exchange ideas

e. ☐   sitting of a group over wine or in talk

■ *ZINGERS*

A. **surd:**

a. ☐ voiceless sound
b. ☐ example of foolishness
c. ☐ suppressed indignation
d. ☐ implied response
e. ☐ expression of incredulity

B. **nuncupative:**

a. ☐ harboring lust
b. ☐ declining rapidly in health
c. ☐ not written
d. ☐ expressing strong interest in financial gain
e. ☐ suppressing sexual desire

Test
FIFTY-NINE

1. The film director sued for the right to **expurgate** his biography prior to its publication.

a. ☐ give final approval to
b. ☐ examine contents of
c. ☐ change contents of
d. ☐ improve quality of
e. ☐ remove objectionable matter from

2. Much to my surprise, once over my shyness, I found I had become **garrulous.**

a. ☐ habitually talkative
b. ☐ overly aggressive

c. ☐ forceful in manner

d. ☐ given to making friends

e. ☐ obnoxious in manner

3. After all the coaching given the candidate before the campaign, she still proved incapable of a **laconic** reply to questions put to her by interviewers.

a. ☐ appropriate

b. ☐ using few words

c. ☐ understandable by everyone

d. ☐ intended to be beneficial

e. ☐ intended to attract support

4. By the final meeting of the convention, Hawkins had firmly established herself as a rising star and become the **cynosure** of all eyes.

a. ☐ object of curiosity

b. ☐ person perceived as evil

c. ☐ person offering promise as a political leader

d. ☐ center of interest

e. ☐ person perceived as a strong competitor

5. I believe a planting of **bracken** will prove attractive in almost any part of the garden.

a. ☐ type of alpine plant

b. ☐ variety of marigold

c. ☐ dwarf evergreen cranberry

d. ☐ Spanish moss

e. ☐ type of large fern

6. The story really becomes interesting after the innocent girl has been transformed into a **fay.**

    a. ☐ fairy

    b. ☐ witch

    c. ☐ evil spirit

    d. ☐ goddess

    e. ☐ seductress

7. Unexpectedly, Peter's **hauteur** proved effective in dealing with his clients.

    a. ☐ sarcasm

    b. ☐ educated speech

    c. ☐ haughtiness of manner

    d. ☐ high-pitched voice

    e. ☐ display of a high degree of intelligence

8. Despite repeated efforts by our team of scientists, we failed to obtain sharply defined color photographs of an **aureole.**

    a. ☐ rapid sequence of contraction and dilation of a blood vessel

    b. ☐ ring around the sun or moon

    c. ☐ earlike minor appendage of a chamber of the heart

    d. ☐ vibratory action of membranes of the inner ear

    e. ☐ vibratory action of bones of the inner ear

9. What does Dave think he gains by taking advantage of every chance to **jape?**

    a. ☐ ask annoying questions

    b. ☐ show off learning

    c. ☐ dominate a discussion

    d. ☐ jest

    e. ☐ use objectionable language

10. Our department boasts at least one person who can be described justifiably as a **polymath.**

  a. ☐ person of broad experience in life

  b. ☐ person interested in intellectual matters to the exclusion of everything else

  c. ☐ person with knowledge of a great many subjects

  d. ☐ person working in all or almost all branches of mathematics

  e. ☐ person whose work bridges practical and theoretical aspects of mathematics

■ *ZINGERS*

A. **pericope:**

  a. ☐ roundabout way of speaking

  b. ☐ interruption of normal sequence of muscular contraction and relaxation

  c. ☐ open space surrounded by columns

  d. ☐ contraction of a word by omitting one or more sounds from the beginning or end

  e. ☐ extract from a book

B. **reify:**

  a. ☐ restore to godlike status

  b. ☐ bring back to profitable condition

  c. ☐ realize predicted benefits

  d. ☐ convert into a concrete thing

  e. ☐ make public again

Test
SIXTY

1. By late summer, the Middle East had once again become a **tinderbox.**

   a. ☐ source of trouble

   b. ☐ source of annoyance

   c. ☐ potentially explosive place

   d. ☐ likely site for revolutions

   e. ☐ likely area for concern

2. Many newspaper readers believe some of our public officials have fallen into an **abyss.**

   a. ☐ trap set to catch wrongdoers

   b. ☐ hole so deep it appears bottomless

   c. ☐ state of absentmindedness

   d. ☐ habit of neglect

   e. ☐ condition of hopelessness

3. At the time the **cryptic** message attracted a great deal of attention.

   a. ☐ extremely offensive

   b. ☐ conveying information concerning a death or burial

   c. ☐ obviously important

   d. ☐ concealing meaning in a puzzling way

   e. ☐ expressing contempt

4. A weekend spent indoors with wall-to-wall football had left her **sated** with television.

   a. ☐ moved to feelings of extreme revulsion

   b. ☐ thoroughly satisfied

c. ☐ moved to open opposition

d. ☐ suffering symptoms of sickness

e. ☐ weary as a result of more than enough

5. The firm can no longer overlook **blatant** errors Meryl makes in computation.

a. ☐ attracting attention in a very obvious way

b. ☐ serious in effect

c. ☐ minor in effect

d. ☐ extremely harmful

e. ☐ deliberately hidden

6. Once again students were treated to an inappropriate **sally** by the lecturer.

a. ☐ mild insult

b. ☐ lively or witty remark

c. ☐ strong attack of a personal nature

d. ☐ vulgar joke

e. ☐ challenge

7. Church officials met to take up the charge of **sacrilege.**

a. ☐ loss of faith by a church minister

b. ☐ improper behavior by a minister

c. ☐ damage to something considered sacred

d. ☐ improper withholding of a sacrament

e. ☐ improper use of church property

8. **Sinistrality** was long considered a sign of deviousness, even criminality.

a. ☐ inability to look someone in the eye

b. ☐ wearing clothing of dark color

c. ☐ avoidance of openness in dealing with others

d. ☐   left-handedness

e. ☐   irregularity of church attendance

9. Eskimos have no present use for an **umiak** except as a means of recalling their former way of life.

a. ☐   house made of blocks of snow

b. ☐   dog sled with wooden runners

c. ☐   hand tool used in scraping hides

d. ☐   stretcher for curing hides

e. ☐   skin-and-wood open boat

10. **Tarantism** was seen in southern Italy over a period of two centuries.

a. ☐   cult worship of the tarantula

b. ☐   uncontrollable mania to dance

c. ☐   reliance on edible tuberous roots as a mainstay of human diet

d. ☐   use of passenger vehicles pulled by humans

e. ☐   intolerance of foreign traders

■ *ZINGERS*

A. **circinate:**

a. ☐   in the manner of a sorceress

b. ☐   rolled up with the apex in center

c. ☐   bounded on all sides

d. ☐   enchanting in manner

e. ☐   resembling a spiral

B. **ulotrichous:**

a. ☐   having wavy hair

b. ☐   losing hair

c. ☐   having straight hair

d. ☐   promoting growth of hair

e. ☐   having wooly hair

Test
SIXTY-ONE

1. Ethel's friends marvel at her remarkable **acumen** in business matters.

a. ☐   success

b. ☐   ability to manage

c. ☐   ability to predict the future

d. ☐   sensitivity to the feelings of others

e. ☐   superior mental acuteness

2. For the life of me, I don't know whether I can put up with his **folderol** any longer.

a. ☐   effeminate manner

b. ☐   tricky behavior

c. ☐   foolish talk

d. ☐   self-praise

e. ☐   interference

3. Cabinet officers will accept an **honorarium** if one is offered.

a. ☐   banquet or other expression of esteem for a retired person

b. ☐   voluntary fee paid for services where custom dictates that no fee is required

c. ☐   customary payment for services rendered by a skilled worker

d. ☐   university degree awarded as a mark of esteem

e. ☐   retirement gift after long service to an institution

4. **Haggis,** for anybody born outside Scotland, is at best an acquired taste.

a. ☐   dish made from sheep's heart, liver, and lungs, seasoned and cooked in a skin made from a sheep's stomach

b. ☐   dish made from lamb's stomach and pancreas, seasoned and cooked in a skin made from a lamb's intestine

c. ☐   dish made from calf's sweetbread, seasoned and cooked in a skin made from a calf's stomach

d. ☐   dish of steamed kippers and eggs, served on slices of toasted bread

e. ☐   dish of rendered animal fat and oatmeal, seasoned and cooked in heavy pastry

5. Aware that Robert might turn out to be my **nemesis,** I took care to withhold information that might damage me.

a. ☐   mortal enemy

b. ☐   unreliable informant

c. ☐   source of damaging gossip

d. ☐   person who violates trust

e. ☐   person who inflicts vengeance

6. What we are looking for is a highly conductive **cupreous** junction.

a. ☐   metallic

b. ☐   extremely rigid

c. ☐   flexible

d. ☐   supplying two or more circuits

e. ☐   containing copper

7. Eugenio Pacelli, later Pius XII, served as **nuncio** from 1917 to 1920.

   a. □   public spokesman for the pope

   b. □   chief administrative officer of the papacy

   c. □   diplomatic representative of the pope

   d. □   close confidant of the pope

   e. □   pope's confessor

8. As predicted, objects in the **penumbra** appeared quite distinct.

   a. □   partial shadow

   b. □   area closest to the viewer

   c. □   area farthest from the viewer

   d. □   a color close to brown

   e. □   center of focus

9. The insect has **pilose** legs that distinguish it from other species.

   a. □   segmented

   b. □   covered with hair

   c. □   enclosed in stiff shell

   d. □   four or more

   e. □   slender

10. Reports of an intestinal **mycosis** in Philadelphia proved inaccurate.

   a. □   parasite attacking membranes

   b. □   invasion of worms

   c. □   fungus present in food incompletely digested

   d. □   disease caused by a fungus

   e. □   type of cancer

■ *ZINGERS*

A. **nacre:**

a. ☐   mother-of-pearl

b. ☐   enclosed part of an airplane

c. ☐   buttock

d. ☐   nostril

e. ☐   type of kettledrum

B. **petrosal:**

a. ☐   elongated

b. ☐   saline solution

c. ☐   large pistol formerly used by horsemen

d. ☐   like stone

e. ☐   deriving from petroleum

Test
SIXTY-TWO

1. The author's latest book certainly received no **accolades** from the newspapers.

a. ☐   lukewarm reviews

b. ☐   reviews notable for their literary quality

c. ☐   statements offering sympathy

d. ☐   expressions of praise

e. ☐   unreasonable attacks

2. Psychologists explain the suicide as the inevitable outcome of the painter's futile attempt to **emulate** his father.

a. ☐   break away from

b. ☐   destroy the reputation of

c. ☐ replace

d. ☐ restore the reputation of

e. ☐ imitate in an effort to equal or surpass

3. How he could appear **blasé** in such difficult circumstances strains understanding.

a. ☐ unimpressed because of overfamiliarity

b. ☐ strong in the face of adversity

c. ☐ sternly defiant

d. ☐ suggesting innocence

e. ☐ uncaring for others

4. We listened in silence, fearing that the **denouement** would further damage the government's reputation.

a. ☐ statement of charges by a prosecutor

b. ☐ reply to charges made in a court of law

c. ☐ unraveling of a tangled sequence of events

d. ☐ denunciation of a high official

e. ☐ expression of doubt or distrust

5. She suggested that a **gimlet** would be useful during the next phase of the project.

a. ☐ small magnifier used by jewelers

b. ☐ small rack used to support an item being drilled

c. ☐ small tool used for boring holes

d. ☐ small rotary buffer

e. ☐ small hand tool to polish gems

6. In many societies, a **caul** is taken as a good omen.

a. ☐ part of a fetal membrane, sometimes found on a child's head at birth

b. ☐ infant born with feet appearing first

c. ☐ birth with placenta and fetal membranes intact

d. ☐ multiple birth of healthy offspring

e. ☐ unanticipated delivery of twins

7. Our architect insists a **mansard** will be practical as well as aesthetically pleasing.

a. ☐ structure useful in summer to take advantage of a view

b. ☐ roof with lower and upper parts, the lower having a steeper slope

c. ☐ grand home in the style of an English manor

d. ☐ home with rectangular center structure and wings at the ends built at right angles

e. ☐ structure of three stories or more with large center hall two stories high

8. A **fecund** imagination is essential for the successful writer of fiction.

a. ☐ wide-ranging

b. ☐ slightly offbeat

c. ☐ given to seeing pictures in the mind

d. ☐ fertile

e. ☐ completely unrestrained

9. In later years, Edgar devoted almost every waking hour to **patristics,** a subject he had avoided in graduate school.

a. ☐ study of nineteenth-century nationalist movements

b. ☐ psychological study of the role of parents in family life

c. ☐ study of laws of inheritance

d. ☐ study of the psychological basis for patriotism

e. ☐ study of the writings of the church fathers

10. I find it hard to understand the appearance of **naiads** in poetry written today.

   a. ☐   women of a sultan's harem

   b. ☐   water nymphs

   c. ☐   Roman goddesses

   d. ☐   mythical Greek heroes

   e. ☐   forest spirits

   ■   *ZINGERS*

A. **orphic:**

   a. ☐   arcane

   b. ☐   inducing sleep

   c. ☐   oracular

   d. ☐   telltale

   e. ☐   overbearing

B. **ormolu:** articles made of or decorated with

   a. ☐   gold-colored alloy

   b. ☐   representations of figures from mythology

   c. ☐   glazed ceramic

   d. ☐   heraldic devices

   e. ☐   highly detailed figures

Test
SIXTY-THREE

1. Did she actually say she had never heard such **drivel** before?

   a. ☐   obvious lying

   b. ☐   baby talk

    c. ☐   gross exaggeration

    d. ☐   deliberate distortion

    e. ☐   silly talk

2. Before we could make our way from the supper table, we were forced to sit through yet another **homily,** the second the headmaster had related that day.

    a. ☐   lengthy anecdote intended to show the good character of the speaker

    b. ☐   lecture on moral conduct

    c. ☐   example of homespun humor

    d. ☐   wordy account of heroic behavior

    e. ☐   frightening warning about misconduct

3. As the final course before coffee and brandy, our hostess offered us a delicious **compote.**

    a. ☐   assortment of fresh fruit

    b. ☐   apple tart

    c. ☐   fruit ice

    d. ☐   fruits cooked in syrup

    e. ☐   open-faced fruit pie

4. When we were children, Mother always kept a supply of **balsam** on hand for all of us.

    a. ☐   aromatic ointment for medicinal use

    b. ☐   needles of a conifer, used for stuffing pillows

    c. ☐   salve used for countering effects of bee sting

    d. ☐   mint used for flavoring tea

    e. ☐   salve used to repel insects

5. As they expected, in the chair's opening remarks she **deprecated** every policy of the present leadership.

- a. ☐ explained fully
- b. ☐ implied full agreement with
- c. ☐ expressed disapproval of
- d. ☐ discussed
- e. ☐ asked for full explanation of

6. Al's friends never knew him to be a truly **parsimonious** person.

- a. ☐ free-spending
- b. ☐ generous to the point of folly
- c. ☐ careful in choice of words
- d. ☐ observant of religious practices
- e. ☐ very sparing in use of resources

7. **Primordial** forms of life stir the imagination of anyone with a deep interest in biology.

- a. ☐ unable to produce offspring
- b. ☐ advanced
- c. ☐ produced by mere chance
- d. ☐ first created or developed
- e. ☐ able to produce offspring

8. Who will be responsible for returning the **breviary** to the proper authorities?

- a. ☐ document conferring a privilege from a sovereign
- b. ☐ summation of a legal writ
- c. ☐ book of daily prayers and readings
- d. ☐ list of documents bearing on a lawsuit
- e. ☐ list of cases cited in a legal brief

9. Once again Joel showed his inclination to **confabulate** regardless of the circumstances.

a. ☐ lie deliberately
b. ☐ converse
c. ☐ play the innocent victim
d. ☐ entertain with off-color stories
e. ☐ ask annoying questions

10. When the **jeroboam** arrived at our table, we knew our host intended to spare no expense.

a. ☐ large team of waiters attending a single table
b. ☐ elaborate ice sculpture
c. ☐ crystal dish of caviar sitting in crushed ice
d. ☐ wine bottle holding about four 26-ounce quarts
e. ☐ elaborate display of hors d'oeuvres

■ *ZINGERS*

A. **scaramouch:**

a. ☐ bold adventurer
b. ☐ expert swordsman
c. ☐ braggart
d. ☐ brave patriot
e. ☐ notorious adulterer

B. **ebullition:**

a. ☐ state of continuing gratitude
b. ☐ narrow escape from danger
c. ☐ complete reversal of attitude
d. ☐ resistance to change
e. ☐ sudden violent outburst

Test
SIXTY-FOUR

1. As we anticipated, he looked upon our suggestions with a **jaundiced** eye.

    a. ☐ afflicted with fatigue

    b. ☐ regarding with total distrust

    c. ☐ tending to judge others unfavorably

    d. ☐ thoroughly experienced

    e. ☐ expert in making assessments

2. Although Ron was told by his lawyer not to lose sleep over the matter, it was clear that the law had been **contravened.**

    a. ☐ inadequately thought through

    b. ☐ violated

    c. ☐ totally ignored

    d. ☐ improperly enforced

    e. ☐ hastily adopted

3. After all that has gone on between us through the years, my confidence in you remains **implicit.**

    a. ☐ second to none

    b. ☐ high

    c. ☐ incapable of being put into words

    d. ☐ strong as ever

    e. ☐ absolute

4. In the Titian portrait I have in mind, the male figure wears a **coif.**

    a. ☐ hoodlike cap

    b. ☐ plain black cape

    c. ☐ neckpiece made of fur

d. ☐   judicial robe

e. ☐   chain worn about the neck for supporting a symbol of office

5. Before discussing **elision,** the instructor asked each of us to say, "I saw them on Wednesday."

a. ☐   influence of regional accent in pronouncing words

b. ☐   influence of ethnic background in pronouncing words

c. ☐   omission of a sound or part of a word in pronouncing words

d. ☐   distortion of final consonant sounds

e. ☐   effect of context on the pronunciation of a single word

6. When Chris was a boy, he started a collection of pictures of brilliantly costumed Hungarian **hussars.**

a. ☐   expert swordsmen

b. ☐   armed patriots opposing a despotic regime

c. ☐   sword dancers

d. ☐   lightly armed horsemen

e. ☐   members of national police

7. Anyone who views the statue is struck immediately by the **leonine** head of the lawgiver.

a. ☐   awe-inspiring

b. ☐   resembling a lion

c. ☐   larger than life-size

d. ☐   heroic

e. ☐   beautifully proportioned

8. False rumors of a shortfall in production had the effect of creating a **factitious** demand for beef.

   a. ☐ persistent

   b. ☐ marked by a sudden increase

   c. ☐ frantic

   d. ☐ reckless

   e. ☐ contrived

9. You will find that every faculty department is blessed with the presence and wisdom of its own **panjandrum.**

   a. ☐ pretentious official

   b. ☐ expert in parliamentary procedure

   c. ☐ judge of customs and manners

   d. ☐ know-it-all

   e. ☐ person who takes pleasure in breaking rules

10. Are you aware that Tanaka is the son of a **sansei?**

   a. ☐ descendant of Japanese warrior class

   b. ☐ expert performer on Japanese guitar

   c. ☐ member of the Japanese royal family

   d. ☐ grandchild of Japanese immigrants to the United States

   e. ☐ expert in Japanese feudal history

■ *ZINGERS*

A. **cubeb:**

   a. ☐ three-dimensional optical illusion

   b. ☐ accurate insight offered by a child

   c. ☐ pet aversion

   d. ☐ medicated cigarette

   e. ☐ illicit activity

B. **dimity:**

a. ☐ thin cotton fabric woven with raised stripes or checks
b. ☐ open ornamental fabric of cotton or wool
c. ☐ plain white unprinted cotton cloth
d. ☐ open cotton cloth used for needlework
e. ☐ striped cotton material with puckered surface

Test
SIXTY-FIVE

1. Do you really mean to suggest that his record shows him to be a complete **nonentity?**

a. ☐ untrained person
b. ☐ unknown person
c. ☐ person of no importance
d. ☐ untrustworthy person
e. ☐ intellectually inferior person

2. What the child really wanted as a birthday present was a **pinto** pony.

a. ☐ high-spirited
b. ☐ Indian
c. ☐ small and gentle
d. ☐ trained for rounding up cattle
e. ☐ spotted or mottled

3. What the president had in mind was to prevent war and all its **concomitant** suffering.

a. ☐ resulting
b. ☐ following

c. ☐ inevitable

d. ☐ happening together

e. ☐ predictable

4. If you know me as well as I think you do, you will not be surprised to find I will not **demean** myself by offering a defense of my activities in her behalf.

a. ☐ lower in dignity

b. ☐ pardon

c. ☐ raise in esteem

d. ☐ praise

e. ☐ explain

5. Not for a moment did anyone **impugn** the colonel's actions.

a. ☐ call in question

b. ☐ approve

c. ☐ discuss impartially

d. ☐ try to influence

e. ☐ combat

6. Serious problems can arise when food is not thoroughly **masticated.**

a. ☐ digested

b. ☐ chewed

c. ☐ cooked before serving

d. ☐ washed before cooking

e. ☐ warmed before serving

7. Mistaken labeling of a **graticule** can cause rejection of the published map.

a. ☐ indication of the scale of a map

b. ☐ name of the type of projection on which a map is based

211

c. ☐ representation of the points of the compass

d. ☐ indication of topographic elevations and depressions

e. ☐ grid on a map representing parallels and meridians

8. Many politicians owe their success to long years of practice in the art of **flummery.**

a. ☐ flowery oration

b. ☐ cooperation with political allies

c. ☐ compromise

d. ☐ empty compliments

e. ☐ deception

9. Apprentice carpenters make many mistakes before they learn to **chamfer** competently.

a. ☐ make a right-angle cut

b. ☐ bevel an edge or corner

c. ☐ construct a plumb wall

d. ☐ cut a large timber

e. ☐ frame a roof

10. Above all it was Rupert's **recreant** behavior before the committee that sealed his fate.

a. ☐ deliberately evasive and deceptive

b. ☐ outrageous

c. ☐ cowardly

d. ☐ openly disrespectful

e. ☐ ungentlemanly

■ *ZINGERS*

A. **shebeen:**

a. ☐   woman claiming to communicate with the dead

b. ☐   daughter of a prostitute

c. ☐   tavern selling liquor illegally

d. ☐   flirtatious barmaid

e. ☐   liquor from an illegal still

B. **redingote:**

a. ☐   artist's coverall or smock

b. ☐   man's hunting coat of brilliant crimson color

c. ☐   cavalryman's tunic reaching to the hips

d. ☐   woman's long coat with cutaway front

e. ☐   child's apron, designed to be worn over a dress

Test
SIXTY-SIX

1. Today, Thomas Gray is known vaguely by many students as the writer of an **elegy.**

a. ☐   funeral oration

b. ☐   poem expressing sorrow

c. ☐   essay on death

d. ☐   novel of country life

e. ☐   memoir of childhood

2. In the end **insidious** rumor brought down his candidacy and sent him into involuntary retirement.

a. ☐   based on partial truth

b. ☐   founded on truth

   c. □ totally false

   d. □ treacherous

   e. □ arising from envy

3. For many years her **Junoesque** beauty, not her superior acting ability, kept audiences enthralled.

   a. □ fresh and childlike

   b. □ youthful

   c. □ large and stately

   d. □ mature and sophisticated

   e. □ unsurpassable

4. As hard as Amy and Charles tried, they could not find an **armoire** worth buying.

   a. □ suit of armor

   b. □ ornamental flower stand

   c. □ decorative trellis

   d. □ coat of arms

   e. □ large wardrobe

5. The committee did not believe the witness when she repeatedly described her decisions as **disinterested.**

   a. □ of concern to no one else

   b. □ unintentional

   c. □ of little importance

   d. □ free of selfish motive

   e. □ routine

6. By the end of the day, I had grown weary of all the **fandango** he had been dishing out.

   a. □ abuse

   b. □ petty complaining

c. ☐   foolishness

d. ☐   insincerity

e. ☐   deliberate exaggeration

7. We spent most of that semester trying to learn how to **parse** a German sentence correctly.

a. ☐   describe grammatically

b. ☐   improve the style of

c. ☐   translate idiomatically

d. ☐   read aloud

e. ☐   construct

8. Most of the laws covering minor traffic offenses have fallen into **desuetude.**

a. ☐   state of general disapproval

b. ☐   state of disuse

c. ☐   condition of unenforceability

d. ☐   judicial rejection on grounds of unconstitutionality

e. ☐   condition of deliberate civil disobedience

9. Who is not charmed by the occasional **oxymoron,** annoyed by its repetitive use?

a. ☐   figure of speech employing marked exaggeration

b. ☐   figure of speech suggesting that the author is profoundly humble

c. ☐   figure of speech imparting human characteristics to other forms of life

d. ☐   figure of speech asserting the opposite of what the author believes

e. ☐   figure of speech combining seemingly contradictory words

10. The great care she usually takes in writing makes the careful reader certain that her frequent **pleonasms** in this work were intentional.

    a. ☐   redundancies

    b. ☐   lapses in grammar

    c. ☐   exaggerations

    d. ☐   mistakes in logic

    e. ☐   chronological errors

■   *ZINGERS*

A. **potlatch:** among American Indians,

    a. ☐   peace pipe

    b. ☐   evening meal

    c. ☐   tribal village

    d. ☐   conference of all nations

    e. ☐   ceremonial feast

B. **prebend:**

    a. ☐   minor village official

    b. ☐   stipend allotted from the income of a cathedral

    c. ☐   drink of ceremonial wine taken before a meal

    d. ☐   debt undertaken in support of a close friend or relative

    e. ☐   inborn trait

Test
SIXTY-SEVEN

1. As Don saw his situation, he was no better than a **peon** in a family business.

   a. ☐ person held in servitude to work off debts

   b. ☐ outsider

   c. ☐ clerk with no opportunity for advancement

   d. ☐ beast of burden

   e. ☐ messenger

2. Jerry used every possible **artifice** to convey the impression that he was a hard worker.

   a. ☐ convincing display

   b. ☐ means at one's disposal

   c. ☐ clever trick

   d. ☐ opportunity

   e. ☐ subtle suggestion

3. When it became apparent that pursuing an artistic career would not lead him out of the **morass** of poverty, he returned to school for training as a physical therapist.

   a. ☐ disgrace

   b. ☐ despair

   c. ☐ unhappy condition

   d. ☐ subculture

   e. ☐ entanglement

4. Much to the amusement of friends who had known Jeff since childhood, a stylish **ascot** soon became his trademark.

   a. ☐ checkered coat

   b. ☐ ivory cigarette holder

217

c. ☐ bow tie

d. ☐ broad scarf looped under the chin

e. ☐ broad-brimmed hat

5. Alston's **mercurial** nature, always the subject of comment, proved decisive in the final selection.

a. ☐ cooperative

b. ☐ erratic

c. ☐ combative

d. ☐ kindly

e. ☐ steady

6. Pendants made of **obsidian** proved popular with tourists early in the season.

a. ☐ polished green stone

b. ☐ yellow stone

c. ☐ volcanic glass

d. ☐ mottled red stone

e. ☐ rounded stone lined with crystals

7. Physicians expressed particular interest in preventing infection among **parturient** women on the ward.

a. ☐ immediately after giving birth

b. ☐ nursing

c. ☐ of advanced age

d. ☐ about to give birth

e. ☐ awaiting surgery

8. **Pediculosis,** although widespread among the troops, did not reduce our combat readiness.

a. ☐ infestation with lice

b. ☐ athlete's foot

c. ☐   ringworm

d. ☐   skin ulcers

e. ☐   type of venereal disease

9. Almost every season brings us a **réchauffé** of their tired views on modern marriage.

a. ☐   strong rebuttal

b. ☐   vigorous defense

c. ☐   careful reexamination

d. ☐   denunciation

e. ☐   rehash

10. Their editorial policies **posit** a never-ending struggle between totalitarianism and democracy.

a. ☐   disregard

b. ☐   assume as a fact

c. ☐   systematically explore

d. ☐   reject as illogical

e. ☐   overlook

■   *ZINGERS*

A. **avatar:**

a. ☐   incarnation of a deity in human form

b. ☐   embodiment of opposing forces of good and evil in a single deity

c. ☐   ultimate perfection of a spirit before reincarnation

d. ☐   continuing struggle for control of a human being throughout life

e. ☐   search by a human being for full self-realization

B. **pococurante:**

a. ☐ minor annoyance

b. ☐ governess

c. ☐ uncaring person

d. ☐ ill-behaved child

e. ☐ peccadillo

Test
SIXTY-EIGHT

1. I am certain Murphy will not **bungle** the job if we give him the appointment.

a. ☐ leave incomplete

b. ☐ forget to do

c. ☐ turn down

d. ☐ fail to understand thoroughly

e. ☐ botch

2. **Illusory** longings may lead inevitably to disappointment, but what is life without them?

a. ☐ exaggerated

b. ☐ high

c. ☐ childish

d. ☐ parental

e. ☐ deceptive

3. The **heady** news that she had won the competition made it easier for Emily to turn at once to her next assignment.

a. ☐ unexpected

b. ☐ previously predicted

c. ☐ expected by all

d. ☐ exhilarating

e. ☐ widely acclaimed

4. To our surprise, by the time Henry turned twenty-one, he had become a **fop.**

a. ☐ person of conservative beliefs

b. ☐ deeply disillusioned person

c. ☐ man excessively concerned about his personal appearance

d. ☐ person completely lacking in ambition

e. ☐ person without interest in intellectual matters

5. After years of operating in a world of petty **cabals,** Jon left academia for a career in social work.

a. ☐ jealousies

b. ☐ secret plots

c. ☐ intellectual disputes

d. ☐ rivalries

e. ☐ political causes

6. We knew so little of his personal habits that the real reason for his **florid** complexion escaped all of us.

a. ☐ reddish

b. ☐ unhealthy

c. ☐ pale

d. ☐ showing lack of exposure to sunlight

e. ☐ showing effects of dissipation

7. No one can recall just how it happened, but Jane clearly had become a **pariah.**

    a. ☐   person of great reputation

    b. ☐   person with ability to prophesy accurately

    c. ☐   judge of social behavior

    d. ☐   person of highest importance

    e. ☐   social outcast

8. Some people are not aware that *farad* is an **eponym.**

    a. ☐   unit of electrical measurement

    b. ☐   universally recognized term

    c. ☐   example of scientific precision

    d. ☐   name derived from a person's name

    e. ☐   example of personification

9. During the **peroration,** practically nobody was paying attention.

    a. ☐   brief introduction by a master of ceremonies

    b. ☐   introductory part of a speech

    c. ☐   last part of a speech

    d. ☐   appeal for funds by a speaker

    e. ☐   commentary on a speech by a panel of discussants

10. In days gone by, a **petard** provided a means for freeing friends imprisoned in a castle.

    a. ☐   bomb used to blow in a gate or door

    b. ☐   small boat propelled by oars

    c. ☐   catapult used for hurling great stones

    d. ☐   battering ram

    e. ☐   rope ladder used for scaling walls

■ *ZINGERS*

A. **scarify:**

a. ☐ frighten severely

b. ☐ cause to turn deep red

c. ☐ pain by severe criticism

d. ☐ cause to swell

e. ☐ decimate

B. **prolegomenon:**

a. ☐ summary

b. ☐ introduction

c. ☐ context

d. ☐ textual analysis

e. ☐ exegesis

Test
SIXTY-NINE

1. He saw retirement not as a **terminus** but as the opportunity for a new career.

a. ☐ fulfillment

b. ☐ final point

c. ☐ fixed date for an event

d. ☐ rigid requirement

e. ☐ punishment

2. One unshakable **tenet** saw him through most of his career.

a. ☐ goal

b. ☐ method of evaluation

   c. ☐   process of reasoning

   d. ☐   understanding of people's motives

   e. ☐   principle held by a person

3. By that stage of his life, Jonah no longer took seriously the suggestion that he become a **proselyte.**

   a. ☐   preacher in foreign lands who encourages religious conversion

   b. ☐   lay leader of a religious movement

   c. ☐   enthusiastic adherent of a religion

   d. ☐   person converted from one belief to another

   e. ☐   charismatic religious leader

4. It was the **tedium** of his work that led to a fundamental change in his outlook.

   a. ☐   quality of being wearisome

   b. ☐   demand for perfection

   c. ☐   hopelessness

   d. ☐   repetitious nature

   e. ☐   slow pace

5. The word processor may not prove to be the **talisman** writers long have sought.

   a. ☐   device that invents plots for stories

   b. ☐   automatic storyteller

   c. ☐   laborsaving device

   d. ☐   genie

   e. ☐   something said to be capable of working magic

6. What inspired our troops to make the final, successful charge was a stirring **skirl**.

  a. ☐ war cry

  b. ☐ rapid drum roll

  c. ☐ bugle call to attack

  d. ☐ opening volley of massed artillery

  e. ☐ shrill sound of a bagpipe

7. Do you remember the **slumgullion** we had to put up with day after day in the work camp?

  a. ☐ foul drinking water

  b. ☐ meat stew

  c. ☐ abusive language

  d. ☐ primitive conditions

  e. ☐ harsh treatment

8. As the young musician soon discovered, temptation was a **protean** phenomenon on concert tours.

  a. ☐ overpowering

  b. ☐ difficult to overcome

  c. ☐ taking many forms

  d. ☐ omnipresent

  e. ☐ dangerous

9. What can be better than **raclette** after a day on the ski slopes?

  a. ☐ marinated and roasted lamb in the Swiss style

  b. ☐ Swiss salad of cheese and tomatoes

  c. ☐ Swiss dish of melted cheese served on bread

  d. ☐ cubed cheese and pork sausage in the Swiss style

  e. ☐ potato and onion soup topped with a crust of Swiss cheese

10. The desire to work hard, the only true **sine qua non,** had somehow disappeared.

  a. ☐ discipline

  b. ☐ indispensable condition

  c. ☐ demanding requirement

  d. ☐ indefinable something

  e. ☐ human trait

■ *ZINGERS*

A. **sprachgeföhl:**

  a. ☐ appropriate wording

  b. ☐ ability to translate idiomatically

  c. ☐ eloquence without use of words

  d. ☐ feeling for language

  e. ☐ gift for creating dialogue

B. **propaedeutics:**

  a. ☐ cures effected without medical intervention

  b. ☐ branch of theology treating of the principles of Biblical interpretation

  c. ☐ art of teaching

  d. ☐ body of knowledge preliminary to higher study

  e. ☐ instruction of beginning medical students

Test
SEVENTY

1. Only in the truly fearful does bravery under fire reach its **acme.**

 a. ☐ lowest point

 b. ☐ peak of perfection

 c. ☐ ultimate test

 d. ☐ greatest shame

 e. ☐ exact opposite in nature

2. Everyone agreed the house had been much improved by a **dormer** installed by its previous owner.

 a. ☐ sleeping porch for use in hot weather

 b. ☐ sliding glass door leading to a terrace

 c. ☐ skylight

 d. ☐ small bedroom for guests

 e. ☐ upright window under a gable built out from a sloping roof

3. We tried as hard as we could but were unable to **elicit** an unfavorable response from the witness.

 a. ☐ suppress

 b. ☐ draw out

 c. ☐ prove illegality of

 d. ☐ erase from the record

 e. ☐ cause to deny

4. It was his **obtrusive** behavior that people commented on most frequently.

 a. ☐ usually unhelpful

 b. ☐ troubling

 c. ☐ childish

d. ☐ unpleasantly noticeable

e. ☐ marked by an unwillingness to compromise

5. Bergman's **nonpareil** performance as St. Joan is almost forgotten now.

a. ☐ falling short of expectations

b. ☐ mediocre

c. ☐ unrivaled

d. ☐ excellent

e. ☐ highly emotional

6. Who can fail to be troubled by the **lacunae** in the statement he prepared for the hearings?

a. ☐ missing parts

b. ☐ obvious misstatements

c. ☐ errors in logic

d. ☐ gross exaggerations

e. ☐ apparent evasions

7. The **inanition** of his new novel becomes apparent almost in the first page.

a. ☐ self-centeredness

b. ☐ lack of human insight

c. ☐ emptiness

d. ☐ obtuseness

e. ☐ complexity

8. University students soon grow accustomed to **peripatetic** lecturers.

a. ☐ unable to look directly at people

b. ☐ instructing through asking questions

c. ☐ overly enthusiastic

d. ☐   lacking interest in students

e. ☐   marked by walking about

9. After a few months' membership on the executive committee, I could no longer take the **pharisaical** discussions that dominated every meeting.

a. ☐   openly bigoted

b. ☐   smug

c. ☐   slanderous

d. ☐   meanspirited

e. ☐   hypocritically self-righteous

10. When the *Times* review characterized Fred's novel as pornographic, the immediate **réclame** proved embarrassing.

a. ☐   absence of public disapproval

b. ☐   commercial success

c. ☐   publicity

d. ☐   public outcry

e. ☐   expression of disapproval

■   *ZINGERS*

A. **sciomancy:** divination by

a. ☐   random reading of the works of philosophers

b. ☐   communicating with ghosts of the dead

c. ☐   random drawing of lines or figures

d. ☐   reading of biblical texts

e. ☐   throwing of bones of the dead

B. **scotoma:**

a. ☐   hardening of the brain

b. ☐   birthmark

c. ☐   stonelike feces

d. ☐   vertigo

e. ☐   blind spot

Test
SEVENTY-ONE

1. "Far be it from me," she said, "to **purloin** a letter so personal."

  a. ☐   write

  b. ☐   steal

  c. ☐   read

  d. ☐   save

  e. ☐   discard

2. Who can resist the chance to lead an **opulent** life?

  a. ☐   carefree

  b. ☐   productive

  c. ☐   ostentatiously rich

  d. ☐   happy

  e. ☐   lazy and purposeless

3. In earlier times a living room without a **hassock** or two was unthinkable.

  a. ☐   deep armchair

  b. ☐   embroidered covering for back or arms of a chair

  c. ☐   full-length mirror

  d. ☐   smoking stand

  e. ☐   cushion used as a footstool

4. I must say that what you have brought up is not **germane** to the class discussion.

   a. ☐ essential

   b. ☐ of sufficient importance

   c. ☐ fitting in nature

   d. ☐ closely related

   e. ☐ foreign

5. Can you picture Burton's **dromedary** carrying the great explorer on his final journey to Medina?

   a. ☐ two-humped camel

   b. ☐ Arabian pony

   c. ☐ horse-drawn litter

   d. ☐ one-humped camel

   e. ☐ hearse

6. **Nascent** feelings of distrust between the partners soon resulted in irreparable damage to their business.

   a. ☐ beginning to develop

   b. ☐ justifiable and strong

   c. ☐ groundless but strong

   d. ☐ inevitable

   e. ☐ growing stronger

7. The boy's greatest ambition was to distinguish himself as a **mahout**.

   a. ☐ juggler

   b. ☐ elephant driver

   c. ☐ circus clown

   d. ☐ village magistrate

   e. ☐ lawyer

8. Once the civilized world turned away from its collective responsibility, the **hecatomb** was inevitable.

   a. ☐ downfall of a great city

   b. ☐ wholesale starvation

   c. ☐ sacrifice of many victims

   d. ☐ economic collapse

   e. ☐ widespread plague

9. The cabinetmaker finally refused to sell his elaborate **prie-dieu**
even though he needed the money it would bring.

   a. ☐ wood carving representing an angel

   b. ☐ stand for holding a Bible

   c. ☐ cast of hands in attitude of prayer

   d. ☐ carved mahogany candelabrum

   e. ☐ kneeling desk for prayer

10. Contrary to recommendations of the minority leader, the
Speaker decided it was time to **prorogue** the House of Represen-
tatives.

   a. ☐ discontinue a session of

   b. ☐ individually poll the members of

   c. ☐ order resumption of debate in

   d. ☐ overrule

   e. ☐ order an immediate vote of

■ *ZINGERS*

   A. **durbar:** in India, formerly,

   a. ☐ chief constable

   b. ☐ Hindu religious ascetic

   c. ☐ member of an outlawed Muslim sect

d. ☐   chanter of holy scripture

e. ☐   court of an Indian ruler

B. **funambulist:**

a. ☐   ambulance chaser

b. ☐   habitual liar

c. ☐   tightrope walker

d. ☐   person who skirts the truth

e. ☐   inveterate womanizer

Test
SEVENTY-TWO

1. In that area the Hudson **meanders** through lush green fields, far from the city it soon will serve.

a. ☐   moves quickly

b. ☐   follows a winding course

c. ☐   moves slowly

d. ☐   spreads over its banks

e. ☐   changes course frequently

2. The museum has a large display case filled exclusively with antique **rapiers.**

a. ☐   shields

b. ☐   straight swords used for thrusting

c. ☐   daggers

d. ☐   weapons

e. ☐   battle-axes

3. Surely you will not take into account an occasional **peccadillo** in assessing a candidate for national office.

   a. □ small cigar

   b. □ error in judgment

   c. □ failure to vote for an important bill

   d. □ deviation from one's party line

   e. □ trifling offense

4. A delegation of senior officials of the United Nations sought a **rapprochement** between the two countries.

   a. □ meeting of heads of states

   b. □ combined effort in support of a cause

   c. □ mutual defense pact

   d. □ resumption of harmonious relations

   e. □ cessation of hostilities

5. You must agree that all other matters **pale** beside the accident at Chernobyl.

   a. □ lose color

   b. □ appear promising

   c. □ seem less important

   d. □ assume great importance

   e. □ take precedence

6. Five days out from San Francisco, a **petrel** appeared alongside our ship.

   a. □ type of seabird that flies far from land

   b. □ flying fish

   c. □ naval vessel

   d. □ volcanic island of recent origin

   e. □ whirlpool

7. Never in my life have I met someone so young who could **malinger** convincingly.

   a. ☐ show attentiveness

   b. ☐ tell lies

   c. ☐ impersonate someone

   d. ☐ argue in favor of a cause

   e. ☐ pretend to be ill to avoid duty

8. By then her **oeuvre** was comparable in quality to that of any of her colleagues.

   a. ☐ elaborate egg cookery

   b. ☐ skill in performing

   c. ☐ reputation

   d. ☐ totality of works of an author or artist

   e. ☐ professional standing in an institution

9. In the notes taken during the intake interview, the secretary characterized Joan as a **nullipara.**

   a. ☐ homeless woman

   b. ☐ destitute woman

   c. ☐ woman who has never borne a child

   d. ☐ illiterate woman

   e. ☐ woman without occupational training or skills

10. John finds it restful to spend much of his spare time making **antimacassars.**

   a. ☐ ornamental plant holders meant to be suspended from a ceiling

   b. ☐ coverings for backs and arms of chairs to prevent soiling

   c. ☐ ornamental plant stands

   d. ☐ medieval wooden musical instruments

   e. ☐ model airplanes, ships, etc.

■ *ZINGERS*

A. **scrannel:**

a. ☐   bituminous coal

b. ☐   discarded matter

c. ☐   unsorted

d. ☐   unmelodious

e. ☐   farfetched

B. **sequacious:**

a. ☐   wordy

b. ☐   coherent

c. ☐   lagging far behind

d. ☐   in correct order

e. ☐   immediately following

Test
SEVENTY-THREE

1. It did not take her long to become a **wary** politician, offering information to the press only when necessary.

a. ☐   obsessed with fear

b. ☐   fully experienced

c. ☐   typical

d. ☐   given to caution

e. ☐   evasive

2. While the appliance had many outstanding features, she ultimately rejected it because it was so **unwieldy.**

a. ☐   limited in applications

b. ☐   inefficient

c. ☐   expensive to operate

d. ☐   difficult to use

e. ☐   impractical

3. In that country, political trials are a **travesty** of justice.

a. ☐   open display

b. ☐   grotesque imitation

c. ☐   procedure conducted in secrecy

d. ☐   complete denial

e. ☐   primitive representation

4. Despite repeated and urgent requests, he would not **vouchsafe** a reply to my question.

a. ☐   grant as a favor

b. ☐   answer in confidence

c. ☐   endorse officially

d. ☐   authorize

e. ☐   respond favorably

5. In interviewing potential members of her staff, she gave full consideration to all candidates except for those few who gave **unctuous** replies to her questions.

a. ☐   excessively flattering

b. ☐   poorly thought-out

c. ☐   obviously untrue

d. ☐   incompletely expressed

e. ☐   self-serving

6. His **tumescent** oratory on the Senate floor had little effect on the votes of his colleagues.

a. ☐   delivered with great conviction

b. ☐   marked by personal attacks

c. ☐ excessively inflated

d. ☐ alternately rising and falling in sound

e. ☐ flattering

7. I am certain that when I saw Sister Maria in front of the cathedral, she was wearing her **wimple.**

a. ☐ nun's full outdoor costume

b. ☐ nun's headcloth worn drawn around the neck and chin

c. ☐ religious medal

d. ☐ rain cloak worn over nun's outdoor costume

e. ☐ nun's costume worn within a convent

8. After days of waiting, the knight was led by his captors to a leader **yclept** Roderick.

a. ☐ under the command of

b. ☐ acting for

c. ☐ senior to

d. ☐ associated with

e. ☐ called by the name of

9. Some of the men arrived in opera hats, but the guest of honor wore his customary **trilby.**

a. ☐ beret

b. ☐ peaked military cap

c. ☐ fez

d. ☐ soft felt hat with indented crown

e. ☐ decorated skullcap

10. The public park was financed by a group that organized a **tontine** for the purpose.

a. ☐ scheme for raising money by annual contributions plus interest earned over a selected number of years, with contributions reduced each year until the desired sum is realized

b. ☐ insurance policies on the lives of contributors who name the same public institution as beneficiary

c. ☐ annuity funded by subscribers and paid to the last surviving subscriber

d. ☐ privately organized lottery with limited number of participants

e. ☐ group purchase of a great number of state-run lottery tickets with prize money received paid to a public institution

■ *ZINGERS*

A. **teratology:**

a. ☐ literary study in four parts
b. ☐ scientific study of spiders
c. ☐ account of military invasion of a country
d. ☐ scientific study of monstrosities
e. ☐ scientific study of soil types

B. **zugzwang:** in chess, a situation which a player

a. ☐ sacrifices a piece in order to gain an advantage in a subsequent move

b. ☐ must choose among disadvantageous moves

c. ☐ offers his opponent a chance to capture a piece that will expose the opponent to checkmate

d. ☐   sacrifices a minor piece to improve board position

e. ☐   makes a series of rapid moves to put his opponent off balance

Test
SEVENTY-FOUR

1. In an understaffed department, there is no way to hide a **sluggard.**

a. ☐   person who is given to telling stories

b. ☐   person whose actions intimidate others

c. ☐   person who refuses to cooperate

d. ☐   person who steals ideas

e. ☐   habitually lazy person

2. For the life of me, I cannot **fathom** his motives in this affair.

a. ☐   explore

b. ☐   find justification for

c. ☐   oppose on logical grounds

d. ☐   understand thoroughly

e. ☐   find the origin of

3. At first I saw her argument as **tenable,** but most of the others disagreed with me.

a. ☐   carrying great weight

b. ☐   worthy of attention

c. ☐   reflecting much thought

d. ☐   capable of being defended

e. ☐   probably correct

4. The attending physicians all considered the infant **viable.**

   a. ☐   fully responsive to stimuli

   b. ☐   capable of living

   c. ☐   capable of taking nourishment

   d. ☐   fully developed

   e. ☐   partially responsive to stimuli

5. As we looked down from the **vertiginous** heights, we finally understood our achievement fully.

   a. ☐   causing dizziness

   b. ☐   rising to great altitude

   c. ☐   difficult to climb

   d. ☐   challenging

   e. ☐   life-threatening

6. When Sean received his first month's pay, he went out immediately and bought his first **ulster.**

   a. ☐   hunting jacket

   b. ☐   suit made of tweed

   c. ☐   long loose overcoat

   d. ☐   knitted sweater carrying the colors of a sports team

   e. ☐   dinner jacket

7. At first she was fascinated by the suggestion that she might enjoy a career in **silviculture.**

   a. ☐   breeding of game fish

   b. ☐   cultivation of forest trees

   c. ☐   breeding of domesticated animals

   d. ☐   branch of sociology dealing with rural populations

   e. ☐   study of the environment of woodland animals

8. The party's **tortuous** legislative tactics surprised only the most naive.

   a. ☐ carelessly prepared

   b. ☐ designed to generate distrust

   c. ☐ based on popular beliefs

   d. ☐ constructed for selfish purposes

   e. ☐ devious

9. The **sophistry** of the arguments he advances so eloquently becomes immediately apparent to careful readers.

   a. ☐ profound and admirable wisdom

   b. ☐ intellectual challenge

   c. ☐ difficulty of understanding

   d. ☐ subtle and perhaps misleading reasoning

   e. ☐ indisputable correctness

10. Our **soigné** chairman almost looked out of place at the meeting he called to hear complaints of members of the junior faculty.

   a. ☐ well-groomed

   b. ☐ smiling

   c. ☐ aging

   d. ☐ self-confident

   e. ☐ apparently unconcerned

■ *ZINGERS*

A. **transpicuous:**

   a. ☐ beyond perception

   b. ☐ conceived elsewhere

   c. ☐ of plaintive quality

   d. ☐ admitting maximum passage of light without distortion

   e. ☐ clearly understood

B. **tantras:** Hindu or Buddhist

  a. ☐ lamentations for the dead

  b. ☐ mystical and magical writings

  c. ☐ ecstatic trances

  d. ☐ representations of deities

  e. ☐ meditations

Test
SEVENTY-FIVE

1. No one suggested that the painkiller was anything more than a useful **expedient.**

  a. ☐ first step in medical treatment

  b. ☐ substance that speeds recovery from illness

  c. ☐ substance that relieves anxiety before surgery

  d. ☐ means to an end

  e. ☐ quickener of perceptions

2. The wooden **palisade** they are building may be strong enough to last for many years.

  a. ☐ garden structure for storing tools

  b. ☐ raised garden bed for growing plants

  c. ☐ fence of pointed poles forming an enclosure

  d. ☐ structure offering shelter for mountain climbers

  e. ☐ cage for animals in a zoo

3. It was said that staff members felt they were required to **genuflect** before addressing the director.

  a. ☐ bend the knees as in worship

  b. ☐ weigh words carefully

    c. ☐   appear appreciative of a favor

    d. ☐   prepare answers for every question that may be asked

    e. ☐   request permission

4. We can find no way to accommodate the **parochial** attitudes reflected in letters we receive from our readers.

    a. ☐   relating to a particular religious belief

    b. ☐   of narrow scope

    c. ☐   closed to discussion

    d. ☐   private in nature

    e. ☐   deeply held

5. In the speech Louis is planning, he intends to make a strong appeal to **disaffected** employees.

    a. ☐   untouched by personal ambitions

    b. ☐   motivated by selfish concerns

    c. ☐   disloyal

    d. ☐   unmotivated

    e. ☐   threatened with dismissal

6. Travelers are advised that **cumshaw** still works like magic in that part of the world.

    a. ☐   a tip

    b. ☐   an instance of courteous behavior

    c. ☐   a kind word

    d. ☐   a sign of respect given to shop employees

    e. ☐   an act of kindness to strangers

7. Neither attorney was interested in a change of **venue** until just before the trial date.

    a. ☐   judicial procedure relating to conduct of a trial

    b. ☐   process for selecting a jury

c. ☐ place in which a trial is held

d. ☐ type of court designated to conduct a trial

e. ☐ size of jury required for a trial

8. A list of **corrigenda** has not yet been received even though one was promised.

a. ☐ planned improvements in mechanical design

b. ☐ dangerous defects

c. ☐ areas of disagreement

d. ☐ misinterpretations

e. ☐ errors to be corrected

9. It was reported to us that they were not caught **in flagrante delicto.**

a. ☐ in open violation of custom

b. ☐ in opposition to direct instructions

c. ☐ in a conspiracy to commit a crime

d. ☐ in the very act of committing an offense

e. ☐ in a plot to undermine religious authority

10. Dawn Hall was established originally as an **eleemosynary** educational institutional.

a. ☐ serving adolescent girls

b. ☐ supported by charity

c. ☐ serving students of a religious sect

d. ☐ intended primarily for vocational training

e. ☐ intended primarily for preparing students for the ministry

■ *ZINGERS*

A. **solfatara:**

a. ☐   volcanic vent giving off gases and steam

b. ☐   practice exercise for singers

c. ☐   preparation of dangerous chemical compounds

d. ☐   fate of mankind

e. ☐   use of syllables to denote the tones of a musical scale

B. **parthenogenesis:**

a. ☐   miraculous intervention to save lives

b. ☐   disputed account of the writing of a literary work

c. ☐   reproduction by development of an egg without fertilization

d. ☐   production of a counterfeit work of art

e. ☐   account of the origin of the universe

Test
SEVENTY-SIX

1. I believe that in the end there will be no reason to **gainsay** Ms. Egner's technical ability.

a. ☐   verify

b. ☐   oppose

c. ☐   discuss

d. ☐   speak favorably of

e. ☐   deny

2. Once the police terminate their investigation, any further search you and I undertake is sure to be **fraught with** danger.

   a. ☐ completely free of

   b. ☐ accompanied by

   c. ☐ relatively free of

   d. ☐ defeated by the threat of

   e. ☐ overly occupied with avoiding

3. Once the economy began to show signs of weakness, three major steel companies formed a **cartel.**

   a. ☐ joint operation to reduce costs of production

   b. ☐ joint distribution organization to reduce costs

   c. ☐ combination of business firms to avoid competition

   d. ☐ uniform pricing structure

   e. ☐ trade association

4. Jim spent so much time satisfying his **gregariousness** that he fell far behind in his work.

   a. ☐ love of food and drink

   b. ☐ love of sports

   c. ☐ need for healthful exercise

   d. ☐ inclination to associate with others

   e. ☐ yearning for foreign travel

5. According to one account, the **bursar** exercised extraordinary powers during that period.

   a. ☐ personnel officer

   b. ☐ writer of promotional materials

   c. ☐ production manager

   d. ☐ hospital administrator

   e. ☐ financial officer of a university

6. No circus worthy of the name can afford to be without a **cal-liope.**

   a. ☐   group of clowns

   b. ☐   sideshow exhibiting people and animals with abnormal physical characteristics

   c. ☐   musical instrument resembling an organ

   d. ☐   team of acrobats performing feats of daring

   e. ☐   team of performing animals

7. While most of us questioned his character, by no means did anyone describe him as a **miscreant.**

   a. ☐   vicious person

   b. ☐   sexual pervert

   c. ☐   felon

   d. ☐   liar

   e. ☐   disloyal person

8. Pay close attention to anyone who threatens you with **defenestration.**

   a. ☐   intentional breaking of a person's eardrums

   b. ☐   act of throwing a person or thing out of a window

   c. ☐   castration

   d. ☐   torture with a cattle prod

   e. ☐   prolonged imprisonment marked by deprivation of human contact

9. As Clarissa worked, she came to the realization that the novel would surely be her **magnum opus.**

   a. ☐   greatest work

   b. ☐   best-selling work

   c. ☐   final work

d. □ first published work

e. □ definitive autobiographical work

10. **Pointillism,** much in vogue among French Impressionists, is seldom employed by modern artists.

a. □ technique employing oils and watercolors in a single painting

b. □ technique of altering natural forms in a painting to emphasize underlying geometric patterns

c. □ style of portrait painting that emphasizes color and line rather than character of the subject

d. □ technique of crowding a canvas with spots of various colors, which are blended by the viewer's eye

e. □ technique of swirling contrasting colors on a canvas to convey the impression of movement

■ *ZINGERS*

A. **prelapsarian:** pertaining to conditions existing before

a. □ a forgotten incident

b. □ commission of an error of judgment

c. □ neglect of a personal obligation

d. □ recorded history

e. □ the fall of man

B. **verrucose:**

a. □ dilated

b. □ veinlike

c. □ wartlike

d. □ almost truthful

e. □ bearing fruit

Test
SEVENTY-SEVEN

1. Everyone understood that the resupply operation was to be launched **sub rosa.**

  a. ☐   secretly

  b. ☐   as soon as possible

  c. ☐   at night

  d. ☐   without official sanction

  e. ☐   as an emergency measure

2. The pattern of Leo's life up until now makes me feel certain he soon will **revert** to a life of crime.

  a. ☐   decide to abandon

  b. ☐   take up

  c. ☐   return

  d. ☐   react with shame

  e. ☐   show signs of reform

3. By no stretch of the imagination can we describe him as a **sagacious** person.

  a. ☐   highly regarded

  b. ☐   reliable

  c. ☐   showing strong regard for the feelings of others

  d. ☐   of keen judgment

  e. ☐   highly educated

4. Most experts agree nothing will be gained from **resection** at this time.

  a. ☐   surgical removal of part of an organ or bone

  b. ☐   replacement of a constricted or damaged blood vessel

  c. ☐   further surgery

d. □   removal of a tumor

e. □   reattachment of a severed blood vessel

5. We are looking for a commercial artist capable of producing a **variegated** presentation that attracts attention but does not distract from the essential sales message.

a. □   inherently interesting

b. □   striking

c. □   derived from many sources

d. □   appealing to a wide variety of tastes

e. □   diversified in appearance

6. Pamela never acquired a **penchant** for word games and crossword puzzles.

a. □   abhorrence

b. □   ability

c. □   outstanding ability

d. □   necessary interest

e. □   strong inclination

7. In conducting an environmental study, ecologists give full consideration to the **physiology** of the dominant plant species.

a. □   feeding habits

b. □   organic processes

c. □   evolutionary niche

d. □   degree of uniformity

e. □   function

8. In the old days, at roundup time north of San Antonio, no cowboy left the ranch without his **riata.**

a. □   sleeping bag

b. □   emergency ration

251

  c. ☐ large plug of tobacco

  d. ☐ lariat

  e. ☐ wineskin

9. When the Bensons returned from their trip to the Orient, they were proud owners of an antique **samisen.**

  a. ☐ Japanese rice bowl

  b. ☐ Japanese tea service

  c. ☐ three-stringed Japanese guitar

  d. ☐ samurai sword

  e. ☐ woman's formal kimono worn at court

10. Vera will sell her entire collection, with the exception of the valuable **tabard** she had bought on her first trip to England.

  a. ☐ small drum with one head of calfskin

  b. ☐ loose-fitting short coat or cape

  c. ☐ Asian musical instrument resembling a lute

  d. ☐ lapboard

  e. ☐ rolltop desk

■ *ZINGERS*

A. **hakim:** Muslim

  a. ☐ merchant or beggar

  b. ☐ physician or ruler

  c. ☐ landowner or fakir

  d. ☐ manager or attorney

  e. ☐ proprietor or tenant

B. **synecdoche:** figure of speech in which

a. ☐ a name or descriptive term is applied to an object to which it is not literally applicable

b. ☐ initial sounds of words in a phrase are transposed for the purpose of achieving a comic effect

c. ☐ elements of two or more words are combined to produce a novel sense

d. ☐ a part is used for the whole or a whole for the part

e. ☐ a natural sound is used to represent the creature or person that is the source of the sound

Test
SEVENTY-EIGHT

1. The last thing we need is an **ungainly** fashion model in this showroom.

a. ☐ overweight

b. ☐ gum-chewing

c. ☐ awkward-looking

d. ☐ temperamental

e. ☐ knock-kneed

2. My dentist claims that modern techniques she employs can effectively prevent **caries.**

a. ☐ loss of teeth

b. ☐ tooth decay

c. ☐ malformation of teeth

d. ☐ need for false teeth

e. ☐ tooth discoloration

3. In their home everyone is expected to observe the **amenities** so often disregarded in modern living.

a. ☐ patterns of high moral behavior

b. ☐ gestures of respect for elders

c. ☐ table manners

d. ☐ signs of awareness of the feelings of children

e. ☐ polite ways or manners

4. Over time, you may be sure the surface will **abrade** significantly.

a. ☐ discolor

b. ☐ darken

c. ☐ wear away by rubbing

d. ☐ develop nicks and scratches

e. ☐ become extraordinarily smooth

5. Whatever you do, be sure not to **unbosom** yourself in her presence.

a. ☐ dress in an open blouse

b. ☐ make excuses for

c. ☐ claim superiority for

d. ☐ contradict

e. ☐ reveal one's thoughts or feelings

6. Much to my surprise, even our chief designer could find nothing to **cavil** about.

a. ☐ suggest with the intention of helping

b. ☐ add to a discussion

c. ☐ attack indirectly

d. ☐ raise irritating and petty objections

e. ☐ criticize harshly and openly

7. The way he lives encourages most people to regard him as a **troglodyte.**

    a. ☐ health faddist

    b. ☐ cave dweller

    c. ☐ throwback to an earlier time

    d. ☐ religious fanatic

    e. ☐ mentally deranged person

8. I can find no **rubric** that applies precisely to our situation.

    a. ☐ proverb or saying

    b. ☐ established rule or procedure

    c. ☐ formal grammatical analysis

    d. ☐ myth or ancient legend

    e. ☐ mathematical proof

9. During our trip to Greece, we saw the remains of an ancient **stoa.**

    a. ☐ outdoor marketplace

    b. ☐ amphitheater

    c. ☐ ancient sailing vessel

    d. ☐ roofed structure supported by columns

    e. ☐ academy

10. We hope to be able to add a **timbrel** to our collection of old musical instruments.

    a. ☐ tambourine

    b. ☐ flute

    c. ☐ harpsichord

    d. ☐ violin

    e. ☐ horn

■ *ZINGERS*

A. **soutane:**

a. ☐   sustained ballet lift

b. ☐   wry smile

c. ☐   type of mustache

d. ☐   cassock

e. ☐   narrow braid for a cap

B. **majuscule:** written in

a. ☐   imposing style

b. ☐   large letters

c. ☐   sprawling script

d. ☐   capital italics

e. ☐   uncials

Test
SEVENTY-NINE

1. Observers insist that if international relations are to improve, our country's intentions must be perceived as **pacific.**

a. ☐   firm and fair

b. ☐   helpful to others

c. ☐   carefully thought through

d. ☐   clear and wise

e. ☐   conciliatory

2. It is dangerous for officers of the law to ignore acts of **pilferage.**

a. ☐   sexual misconduct

b. ☐   violence committed on members of one's own family

c. □ feuding between neighbors

d. □ petty theft

e. □ destruction of property

3. Upon conclusion of specialized training, Albright was assigned to a **leprosarium.**

a. □ hospital for treatment of leprosy

b. □ medical isolation ward for patients with communicable diseases

c. □ research facility for study of tropical diseases

d. □ research facility for study of butterflies

e. □ research facility for study of small animals

4. You may find the request **risible,** but I am inclined to treat it seriously.

a. □ ordinary

b. □ unjustifiable

c. □ laughable

d. □ meant to be ignored

e. □ inconceivable

5. Tell me about the accident once more, but this time be sure to include all the **lurid** details.

a. □ minor

b. □ horrifying

c. □ causing tears

d. □ relating to acts of heroism

e. □ previously omitted

6. To give rock music its due, it surely provides young people worldwide with a **lingua franca.**

    a. ☐   means of self-expression

    b. ☐   release from tension

    c. ☐   inexpensive and interesting activity

    d. ☐   reason for living

    e. ☐   something resembling a common language

7. Most of the factory employees consider the new rules only a **palliative** for the crushing boredom they experience every day of the week.

    a. ☐   form of payment

    b. ☐   reasonable excuse

    c. ☐   means of diversion

    d. ☐   something that relieves without curing

    e. ☐   way of forgetting

8. Not one member of the staff really believed that the phenomenon was **scrutable.**

    a. ☐   resulting from a chance occurrence in nature

    b. ☐   capable of being understood through close study

    c. ☐   worthy of examination

    d. ☐   readily repeatable

    e. ☐   influenced by presence of observers

9. For the second movement, Mozart wrote a captivating **schottische** that still charms listeners.

    a. ☐   music for a dance resembling a slow polka

    b. ☐   music for a Highland fling

    c. ☐   music for a slow square dance

    d. ☐   music with a strong thematic content

    e. ☐   music conveying a feeling of rustic simplicity and mood

10. Even viewers untrained in art were struck immediately by the **effulgence** of the new work.

a. ☐ care in execution

b. ☐ brilliance in design

c. ☐ radiant splendor

d. ☐ intensity

e. ☐ exuberance

■ *ZINGERS*

A. **synesis:** grammatical construction in which

a. ☐ agreement in meaning is used instead of agreement in form

b. ☐ certain elements are intentionally omitted

c. ☐ certain elements are intentionally repeated

d. ☐ the object of the verb in one clause functions as subject of the verb in the next clause

e. ☐ a modifier is intentionally made ambiguous so that it appears to modify two different elements simultaneously

B. **umbles:**

a. ☐ acts intended to inflict comeuppance

b. ☐ acts of humility

c. ☐ clusters of reproductive organs on moss

d. ☐ animal entrails, used as food

e. ☐ dark spots on the moon

Test
EIGHTY

1. No longer is the population of that country as nearly **homogeneous** as it once was.

   a. ☐   united in political outlook
   b. ☐   uniform throughout
   c. ☐   inclined toward cooperation
   d. ☐   educated to full potential
   e. ☐   politically conservative

2. Once my guests finished the rich **gumbo,** they showed little interest in the remaining courses.

   a. ☐   stew of assorted fish and shellfish
   b. ☐   type of pâté
   c. ☐   vegetable soup thickened with okra pods
   d. ☐   dish of highly seasoned shrimp and rice
   e. ☐   dish of fried chicken with cream sauce

3. Under the **tutelage** of older students, Michael quickly learned to drink impressive quantities of beer.

   a. ☐   example
   b. ☐   encouragement
   c. ☐   sponsorship
   d. ☐   influence
   e. ☐   instruction

4. Without doubt, the condition known as **bulimia** is a far from recent phenomenon.

   a. ☐   abnormal craving for food
   b. ☐   excessive need for praise and recognition
   c. ☐   addiction to harmful drugs

d. □   excessive sexual desire

e. □   abnormal lapses of memory

5. To be sure, no one thus far has characterized him as a **libertine.**

a. □   person devoted to the cause of liberty

b. □   person with little regard for the feelings of others

c. □   person unconcerned with ethical questions

d. □   person who rejects art and literature

e. □   person leading a dissolute life

6. All he longed for was an opportunity to **aestivate** comfortably.

a. □   retire from work

b. □   spend the summer

c. □   devote time to painting

d. □   indulge in contemplation

e. □   attend to personal matters

7. So far as we know, Melissa's **probity** has never before been questioned.

a. □   concern for people

b. □   employment record

c. □   judgment

d. □   integrity

e. □   experimental technique

8. Once the surgeon had cut through the layer of **adipose** tissue, she realized that the damaged organ was beyond repair.

a. □   connecting

b. □   supporting

c. □   fatty

261

d. ☐   diseased

e. ☐   healthy

9. We recall fondly the many evenings we spent together in Ireland, savoring the best **poteen** either of us had ever known.

a. ☐   lamb stew

b. ☐   whiskey from an illicit still

c. ☐   frank conversation

d. ☐   story-telling

e. ☐   intimacy

10. After dinner, in the early years of our marriage, it was my wife's habit to retire to our sitting room and enjoy a **tisane.**

a. ☐   lively gypsy tune

b. ☐   chocolate mint patty

c. ☐   session of lacemaking

d. ☐   beverage made by steeping dried herbs

e. ☐   quiet time

■   *ZINGERS*

A. **retiarius:** Roman

a. ☐   gladiator who used a net to trap an opponent

b. ☐   rule of retribution for crime committed against a citizen

c. ☐   governor of a colony

d. ☐   practice of enforced silence as a punishment

e. ☐   leather pouch suspended from a shoulder

B. **scissile:**

a. ☐   yielding nutritious oil

b. ☐   shaped like a pair of crossed bones

c. ☐   capable of being split easily

d. ☐   not free to move about

e. ☐   easily penetrated

Test
EIGHTY-ONE

1. My **witless** answer to the first question proved decisive in the brief interview.

a. ☐   humorless

b. ☐   sarcastic

c. ☐   incorrect

d. ☐   foolish

e. ☐   ambiguous

2. The **waif** stood outside the department store, where she caught everyone's attention.

a. ☐   abandoned child

b. ☐   lost child

c. ☐   small child

d. ☐   sickly child

e. ☐   frail child

3. Although Bill tried at first to **mollify** me, in the end he abandoned the effort.

a. ☐   encourage

b. ☐   appease

c. ☐   persuade

d. ☐   trick

e. ☐   dissuade

4. Without hesitation we decided to take the **tyke** home with us.

   a. ☐   sickly child

   b. ☐   orphan

   c. ☐   battered child

   d. ☐   lost child

   e. ☐   small child

5. **Indigenous** plants became Anne's specialty early in her career.

   a. ☐   suited to desert regions

   b. ☐   suited to temperate regions

   c. ☐   native

   d. ☐   suited to tropical regions

   e. ☐   suited to mountain regions

6. Dorothy's cook had managed somehow to make leather of what was intended to be **tournedos.**

   a. ☐   filet mignon

   b. ☐   sirloin steak

   c. ☐   porterhouse steak

   d. ☐   small garnished slices of beef fillet

   e. ☐   roast prime ribs of beef

7. By the end of the first hour, there were clear signs that the audience was becoming **restive.**

   a. ☐   restless

   b. ☐   hostile

   c. ☐   enthusiastic

   d. ☐   intensely interested

   e. ☐   partisan

8. The physicians at first were inclined to rule out **lordosis,** but close examination forced them to reconsider.

a. ☐ abnormal forward curvature of the spine

b. ☐ degenerative disease of body tissues

c. ☐ reduction of blood supply to feet and ankles

d. ☐ swelling due to air in body tissues

e. ☐ degeneration of brain tissue

9. The result of all our careful work was a **viscid** fluid that was nearly free of residue.

a. ☐ thin and clear

b. ☐ opaque

c. ☐ thick and gluey

d. ☐ colorless

e. ☐ useful as a lubricant

10. Based on my experience, I doubt that the order she gave is subject to **recision.**

a. ☐ review

b. ☐ cancellation

c. ☐ extension

d. ☐ revision

e. ☐ interpretation

■ *ZINGERS*

A. **lycanthrope:**

a. ☐ person morbidly afraid of insects

b. ☐ person who hates mankind

c. ☐ turncoat

d. ☐ victim of assassination

e. ☐ werewolf

B. **inglenook:**

a. ☐ nook beside an open fireplace

b. ☐ place that affords privacy

c. ☐ quiet fishing stream

d. ☐ sunny opening in deep woods

e. ☐ country cottage

Test
EIGHTY-TWO

1. John's **credulity** always has astounded his friends.

a. ☐ complete honesty

b. ☐ outspokenness

c. ☐ inclination to believe too readily

d. ☐ willingness to confront danger

e. ☐ refusal to take advantage of others

2. Clearly, the **onus** is on the governor to prove he acted in good faith.

a. ☐ political pressure

b. ☐ responsibility

c. ☐ political reality

d. ☐ next move

e. ☐ final argument

3. Only rare ministers can create a **parable** that holds the attention of their congregations.

a. ☐ metaphor intended to illuminate a sermon

b. ☐ sermon on moral behavior

c. ☐ lengthy explanation of a spiritual lesson

d. ☐ imagined narrative designed to illustrate a moral lesson

e. ☐ account of saintly behavior

4. The **motley** crowd that stood before the candidate seemed to take him by surprise.

a. ☐ large and hostile

b. ☐ of varied character

c. ☐ poorly dressed

d. ☐ quiet and unenthusiastic

e. ☐ sullen

5. All the farmer's efforts finally paid off in **friable** soil capable of producing excellent crops.

a. ☐ rich in organic matter

b. ☐ well-drained

c. ☐ fertile

d. ☐ easily crumbled

e. ☐ rich and dark

6. They could find no practical way to **desiccate** the herbs they had collected.

a. ☐ preserve by drying

b. ☐ protect against moisture

c. ☐ reduce to powder

d. ☐ remove unwanted parts from

e. ☐ preserve by freezing

7. My own preference is the **damson,** but only when it is picked at the point of full ripeness.

a. ☐ large yellow apple

b. ☐ small green and brown pear

c. ☐ thin-skinned orange

d. ☐   small spherical watermelon

e. ☐   small dark-purple plum

8. **Flocculent** clouds stood high in the blue sky, as though watching over our picnic.

a. ☐   harmless

b. ☐   disorganized

c. ☐   tuftlike

d. ☐   pure white

e. ☐   tightly connected

9. As we made our way across the **scoria,** the ancient volcano above us looked more and more forbidding.

a. ☐   trees felled by lava flows

b. ☐   nearly cool lava

c. ☐   rough cindery lava

d. ☐   deep chasm in cooled lava

e. ☐   terrain recently covered by lava flow

10. Much to the chemist's surprise, the compound she had developed turned out to be **labile.**

a. ☐   unstable

b. ☐   difficult to manufacture

c. ☐   lacking in practical application

d. ☐   unsuitable for intended use

e. ☐   unoriginal

■ *ZINGERS*

A. **havelock:**

a. ☐   lock of hair just above the forehead

b. ☐   attachment to a cap to protect the back of the neck

c. ☐   long lock of hair worn over the shoulder

d. ☐   bar sliding into a socket to fasten a door

e. ☐   band worn on the head to restrain long hair

B. **velitation:**

a. ☐   throat irritation

b. ☐   lozenge

c. ☐   minor dispute

d. ☐   plush finish for cloth

e. ☐   abrupt change in thought

Test
EIGHTY-THREE

1. No one on the jury fully believed the **infamous** witness, but his testimony nevertheless had its intended effect.

a. ☐   sly and evasive

b. ☐   highly publicized

c. ☐   giving the appearance of deceiving

d. ☐   giving the appearance of exaggerating

e. ☐   deserving a very bad reputation

2. The recipe calls for the addition of **croutons** just before serving.

a. ☐   grated raw vegetables

b. ☐   melted cheeses

c. ☐   assorted herbs

d. ☐   cubes of toasted or fried bread

e. ☐   minced chives

3. In that sect, **ablutions** always are performed after meals.

   a. ☐ ceremonial washing of parts of body

   b. ☐ blessing of food and drink

   c. ☐ prayers of thanksgiving

   d. ☐ periods of meditation

   e. ☐ prayers asking forgiveness for overindulgence

4. Everyone who knew her circumstances considered her **largesse** exceptional.

   a. ☐ plentiful supply of food and drink

   b. ☐ generous gift-giving

   c. ☐ ornate style of dressing

   d. ☐ willingness to compromise

   e. ☐ strict adherence to a code of conduct

5. Anyone who thinks that Oscar's **epigram** suddenly came to him in finished form credits him with more wit than he had.

   a. ☐ tombstone inscription

   b. ☐ book title

   c. ☐ pointed saying

   d. ☐ conclusion to a speech

   e. ☐ chapter title

6. What followed the declaration of martial law can best be described as a **hegira**.

   a. ☐ long period of despair

   b. ☐ emotional expression of relief

   c. ☐ widespread repressed resentment

   d. ☐ general exodus

   e. ☐ restoration of peaceful conditions

7. Her **salutary** advice that we live up to the letter of the law was rejected by a narrow margin.

    a. ☐ based on sound reasoning

    b. ☐ given before leave-taking

    c. ☐ producing a beneficial effect

    d. ☐ well-intentioned

    e. ☐ respectful

8. So many centuries had passed that the **epigraph** was difficult to read and impossible to comprehend.

    a. ☐ inscription

    b. ☐ short commemorative poem

    c. ☐ dedication

    d. ☐ handwritten notation

    e. ☐ explanation of symbols

9. He was the **scion** of a distinguished and well-to-do literary family.

    a. ☐ illegitimate son

    b. ☐ descendant

    c. ☐ adopted son

    d. ☐ oldest living member

    e. ☐ surviving heir

10. Late in the month, they made their first effort to **saponify** the animal fat.

    a. ☐ melt down

    b. ☐ reduce in amount

    c. ☐ make more edible

    d. ☐ eliminate impurities in

    e. ☐ convert into soap

■ *ZINGERS*

A. **plantigrade:**

a. ☐ plant that sends out shoots laterally

b. ☐ three-view architectural drawing

c. ☐ animal that walks on its soles

d. ☐ uninterrupted progress

e. ☐ combined effort toward common objective

B. **golem:** in Jewish legend,

a. ☐ clay figure brought to life

b. ☐ omniscient human fetus

c. ☐ representation of Messiah

d. ☐ object of idolatry

e. ☐ role of a mother

Test
EIGHTY-FOUR

1. When the damning evidence finally was shown to the witness, he sat **agape,** unable to make a sound.

a. ☐ grief-stricken

b. ☐ open-mouthed

c. ☐ staring

d. ☐ forlorn

e. ☐ deeply embarrassed

2. Within our circle of friends, Dennis was the only person who aptly could be called an **anglophile.**

   a. ☐ expert conniver

   b. ☐ student of literature

   c. ☐ one who greatly admires the English

   d. ☐ expert in the study of worms

   e. ☐ expert in fishing

3. Not seen so often anymore is the once-popular **cummerbund.**

   a. ☐ stiff felt hat with a rounded crown

   b. ☐ collapsible top hat

   c. ☐ broad neck scarf looped under the chin

   d. ☐ low shoe that grips the foot at the toe and heel

   e. ☐ sash worn around the waist

4. Once the sturdy **balustrade** had been put in place, we all felt more secure.

   a. ☐ lengthwise structure along the base of a ship

   b. ☐ armrest for a chair

   c. ☐ platform for supporting a mattress

   d. ☐ row of upright posts topped by a rail

   e. ☐ defense against invasion

5. The result of his efforts may accurately be characterized as **cacophony.**

   a. ☐ harsh discordant sound

   b. ☐ uncontrollable confusion

   c. ☐ desired result

   d. ☐ complete agreement among all parties to a dispute

   e. ☐ resumption of hostilities

6. Members of the jury agreed that the **disingenuous** testimony of the principal witness had influenced their verdict.

a. ☐ self-serving
b. ☐ giving a false appearance of candor
c. ☐ factually correct
d. ☐ obviously intended to mislead
e. ☐ openly hostile

7. Veteran members of the symphony orchestra admired the new flutist's **embouchure.**

a. ☐ response to cues from a conductor
b. ☐ ability to achieve subtle tonal qualities
c. ☐ adjustment of the lips to the mouthpiece of a wind instrument
d. ☐ ability to respond to rapid changes in tempo
e. ☐ ability to play as a member of an ensemble

8. When, at the end, they turned to serving **Mammon,** all their previous accomplishments were forgotten.

a. ☐ interests of countries other than one's own
b. ☐ one's own interests
c. ☐ disregard for others as a principle of action
d. ☐ wealth regarded as an evil influence
e. ☐ philosophy suggesting pleasure as the guiding principle of living

9. Outside the door, apparently waiting to be admitted, stood a **homunculus.**

a. ☐ diplomatic courier
b. ☐ minor official
c. ☐ junior clerk

d. ☐   confidential adviser

e. ☐   little man

10. She concerned herself with **iconography** rather than with the techniques used in creating works of art.

a. ☐   conventional images associated with a subject

b. ☐   artistic representation of religious themes

c. ☐   use of works of art for purposes of prayer

d. ☐   identification of artists who have created important works

e. ☐   illustration of themes hostile to religion

■   *ZINGERS*

A. **frisson:**

a. ☐   suggestion

b. ☐   slight fear

c. ☐   presentiment

d. ☐   emotional thrill

e. ☐   slight suspicion

B. **diastrophism:** action of the forces that

a. ☐   caused the fall from Paradise

b. ☐   establish weather patterns on Earth

c. ☐   cause natural disasters

d. ☐   bring on war

e. ☐   deform Earth's crust

Test
EIGHTY-FIVE

1. From then on, his reputation as a **seer** was permanently impaired.

    a. ☐   political leader

    b. ☐   prophet

    c. ☐   scout

    d. ☐   economic analyst

    e. ☐   expert lawyer

2. Mastery of Russian is considered **peripheral** to Joan's present job.

    a. ☐   of no importance

    b. ☐   of diminishing importance

    c. ☐   of minor importance

    d. ☐   of growing importance

    e. ☐   of great importance

3. We believe most people were misled by the **semblance** of integrity they perceived in him.

    a. ☐   slight sign

    b. ☐   total absence

    c. ☐   ambiguous impression

    d. ☐   clear evidence

    e. ☐   outward appearance

4. I was dismayed to discover that the boy had been **morose** during most of the years he spent at boarding school.

    a. ☐   incapable of concentrating

    b. ☐   isolated from friends

    c. ☐   gloomy

d. ☐   unchallenged intellectually

e. ☐   bored

5. After Anne's residency, she gave thought to specializing in **physiatry.**

a. ☐   understanding of bodily processes

b. ☐   art of healing

c. ☐   family medicine

d. ☐   diagnosis and treatment of disease by physical and mechanical means

e. ☐   diagnosis and treatment of mental, emotional, and behavioral disorders

6. What the Eskimo child wanted most of all were new **mukluks.**

a. ☐   combs made of walrus tusks

b. ☐   sealskin mittens

c. ☐   harpoons

d. ☐   sealskin boots

e. ☐   sealskin headdresses

7. Soon after the accident victim was brought to the emergency room, physicians knew they were dealing with a case of **hemiplegia.**

a. ☐   paralysis of the upper part of the body

b. ☐   paralysis of the lower half of the body

c. ☐   impairment of the central nervous system

d. ☐   impairment of half of the brain

e. ☐   paralysis of a lateral half of the body

8. The minister's **heterodox** views caused consternation among some members of the congregation.

    a. ☐ contrary to an accepted standard

    b. ☐ radical

    c. ☐ unacceptable

    d. ☐ liberal

    e. ☐ adhering strictly to religious teachings

9. Once the **penstock** was in place and checked out, the system was ready to operate.

    a. ☐ chute used to direct movement of cattle

    b. ☐ breeding chamber for bacteria

    c. ☐ gate for regulating flow of water

    d. ☐ indicator arm of a measurement apparatus

    e. ☐ control device for heating and cooling apparatus

10. Before prescribing the **febrifuge** drug, the physician conducted a thorough physical examination.

    a. ☐ intended to combat infection

    b. ☐ intended to reduce fever

    c. ☐ intended to control coughing

    d. ☐ intended to reduce anxiety

    e. ☐ intended to reduce blood pressure

■ *ZINGERS*

A. **lusus naturae:**

    a. ☐ offspring of unmarried parents

    b. ☐ optical illusion

    c. ☐ understandable self-deception

    d. ☐ unusual occurrence

    e. ☐ freak of nature

B. **apogee:**

a. ☐ open disagreement

b. ☐ most distant point

c. ☐ close approximation

d. ☐ ultimate goal

e. ☐ hidden motive

Test
EIGHTY-SIX

1. They thought there was no proper way they could **redress** the grievance.

a. ☐ prevent

b. ☐ delay

c. ☐ rectify

d. ☐ obscure

e. ☐ arbitrate

2. He quickly recognized my initial response as an attempt to **rationalize** my predicament.

a. ☐ explain clearly

b. ☐ get out of

c. ☐ get to the bottom of

d. ☐ lay the blame for

e. ☐ offer a reasoned but false explanation of

3. All we need now is a **shim** or two to complete the installation.

a. ☐ thin wedge used to make parts fit

b. ☐ flexible rubber coupling

c. ☐ sharp knife blade

    d. □   fastener

    e. □   coat of paint

4. In disadvantaged areas of the world, **recrudescent** discontentment never comes as a surprise.

    a. □   ever-increasing

    b. □   breaking out again

    c. □   barely concealed

    d. □   deep and sharp

    e. □   uncontrollable

5. No one in a position of authority claims that the man has been a **quisling.**

    a. □   traitor

    b. □   spy

    c. □   criminal conspirator

    d. □   influence peddler

    e. □   weakling

6. What the public perceived as a **non sequitur** affected the outcome of the election.

    a. □   deliberate exaggeration made in order to deceive

    b. □   intentional misstatement made in order to mislead

    c. □   basic character defect

    d. □   conclusion that does not logically follow from the premises

    e. □   personal attack on a political appointment

7. The scientist decided he would **replicate** his experiment before announcing his results.

    a. □   answer remaining questions

    b. □   refine

c. ☐ repeat

d. ☐ redefine

e. ☐ submit for review

8. I found myself looking forward to the company of friends in my old **purlieu.**

a. ☐ childhood home

b. ☐ workplace

c. ☐ church

d. ☐ playfield

e. ☐ haunt

9. The members of the committee were particularly concerned with the **sequelae** of the affair they were investigating.

a. ☐ political benefits

b. ☐ secondary effects

c. ☐ potential benefits

d. ☐ harmful effects

e. ☐ injuries to innocent people

10. **Sericulture** no longer is their principal interest, even less their principal activity.

a. ☐ development of bacterial cultures

b. ☐ plant breeding

c. ☐ study of blood components

d. ☐ preservation of blood supplies

e. ☐ breeding of silkworms

■ *ZINGERS*

A. **seppuku:**

a. ☐ veneration of ancestors

b. ☐ rules of warfare

c. ☐ code of honorable behavior

d. ☐ hara-kiri

e. ☐ rules of individual combat

B. **pinguid:**

a. ☐ clear

b. ☐ talkative

c. ☐ greasy

d. ☐ dappled

e. ☐ painterly

Test
EIGHTY-SEVEN

1. An **acrimonious** discussion ensued after the committee adjourned.

a. ☐ one-sided

b. ☐ ill-advised

c. ☐ bitter in manner

d. ☐ brief

e. ☐ unproductive

2. **Noxious** fumes from the chemical plant were reported by people who lived nearby.

a. ☐ foul

b. ☐ harmful

c. ☐ sharp

d. ☐ deadly

e. ☐ occurring at night

3. Much to her surprise, she was appointed **ombudsman** for the entire corporation.

  a. ☐ official who investigates complaints to see that they are resolved fairly

  b. ☐ labor arbitrator

  c. ☐ personnel officer

  d. ☐ official who ensures compliance with legal requirements

  e. ☐ public relations officer

4. By no means am I **bemused** by the suggestion that he committed his petty thefts in order to help his parents.

  a. ☐ encouraged

  b. ☐ entertained

  c. ☐ astounded

  d. ☐ relieved

  e. ☐ bewildered

5. At the end of the brief ceremony, the guru gave the initiate a **mantra.**

  a. ☐ shoulder covering worn by members of a secret society

  b. ☐ badge of membership in an organization

  c. ☐ sacred book

  d. ☐ sacred phrase believed to have mystical power

  e. ☐ document affirming membership in a society

6. Pete's **hoary** eyebrows rose quizzically, and he said no more.

  a. ☐ black and bushy

  b. ☐ capable of conveying emotion

   c. ☐ white with age

   d. ☐ capable of causing fear

   e. ☐ impressive

7. Just beyond me I saw a beautiful **grouper.**

   a. ☐ type of bird

   b. ☐ type of fish

   c. ☐ type of insect

   d. ☐ type of plant

   e. ☐ type of spiderweb

8. By then, according to most experts, she had mastered **prosody.**

   a. ☐ prose composition

   b. ☐ letter writing

   c. ☐ art of the personal essay

   d. ☐ literary biography

   e. ☐ study of versification

9. Most observers report that **purdah** is less common today than it once was.

   a. ☐ screening of women from public view

   b. ☐ widows sacrificing themselves on their husbands' funeral pyres

   c. ☐ complete subordination of wives to their husbands' wishes

   d. ☐ child marriage

   e. ☐ infanticide

10. She has more **recondite** facts at her fingertips than anyone else I know.

   a. ☐ precisely stated

   b. ☐ useless

c. ☐   useful

d. ☐   little known

e. ☐   half-forgotten

■   *ZINGERS*

A. **numinous:**

a. ☐   self-congratulatory

b. ☐   transparent

c. ☐   attractive

d. ☐   vague

e. ☐   awe-inspiring

B. **nuncupate:**

a. ☐   desire avidly

b. ☐   declare orally

c. ☐   remove copper from

d. ☐   affirm validity of

e. ☐   alter chemical composition of

Test
EIGHTY-EIGHT

1. Her skill in **repartee** made her admired and feared.

a. ☐   fencing

b. ☐   amusing sparring with words

c. ☐   investigative reporting

d. ☐   choice of words

e. ☐   cross-examination

2. **Inherent** in everything he did was a sense of fair play.

  a. ☐ existing as an essential quality

  b. ☐ absent

  c. ☐ truly admirable

  d. ☐ predominant

  e. ☐ completely visible

3. Inevitably, no matter what was said, he would respond with a **gibe.**

  a. ☐ clever remark

  b. ☐ remark intended to impress

  c. ☐ racial epithet

  d. ☐ remark intended to change the subject

  e. ☐ taunt

4. Her view of life as a **crucible** soon became apparent.

  a. ☐ splendid opportunity

  b. ☐ temporary phase

  c. ☐ severe test

  d. ☐ preparation

  e. ☐ challenge

5. Her complete confession, made in the presence of her attorney and other witnesses, **obviated** further inquiry.

  a. ☐ made unnecessary

  b. ☐ called into question

  c. ☐ ended

  d. ☐ encouraged

  e. ☐ became essential for

6. One prominent critic characterized Evan's fictional style as **flat-ulent.**

   a. □   colorless
   b. □   sparing of words
   c. □   engagingly crisp
   d. □   worthy of praise
   e. □   pretentious

7. In his first book, he used worship of Ra, in Egyptian mythology, as his principal example of **heliolatry.**

   a. □   astrology
   b. □   worship of natural phenomena
   c. □   worship of idols
   d. □   sun worship
   e. □   early astronomy

8. When we examine many of André's current creations, we soon understand that **furbelows** abound in much of what he passes off as classic design.

   a. □   colorful fabrics
   b. □   showy ornaments
   c. □   metallic fabrics
   d. □   mistakes in stitching and finishing
   e. □   cheap tricks

9. According to some, his first symphony was little more than a **pastiche.**

   a. □   instance of plagiarism
   b. □   beginner's stumbling effort
   c. □   commendable effort for a beginner
   d. □   imitative work
   e. □   poorly executed work

10. The **peignoir** she bought had been marked down and was not returnable.

a. ☐ summer dress

b. ☐ bathing suit

c. ☐ loose negligee

d. ☐ short frock

e. ☐ evening gown

■ *ZINGERS*

A. **sangfroid:**

a. ☐ calmness in difficulty or danger

b. ☐ cold-bloodedness

c. ☐ complete evasiveness

d. ☐ coolness in personal relations

e. ☐ complete openness

B. **reliquiae:**

a. ☐ minor bequests to surviving family members

b. ☐ personal effects of a dead person

c. ☐ ancient artifacts

d. ☐ fossil remains of plants and animals

e. ☐ paragraphs of a will covering minor bequests

Test
EIGHTY-NINE

1. Why think about the **millennium** when there is enough to interest us at present?

  a. ☐ ultimate worldwide conflict

  b. ☐ destruction of life by severe changes in the natural environment

  c. ☐ future time of human perfection and great happiness

  d. ☐ disarmament and international peace

  e. ☐ revelation of divine truth

2. The debutantes were **resplendent** in ball gowns purchased for the occasion.

  a. ☐ suitably dressed

  b. ☐ brilliant with color

  c. ☐ beautifully dressed

  d. ☐ extremely attractive

  e. ☐ expensively dressed

3. The **reticent** witness offered little of value to explain what the investigators had already found.

  a. ☐ marked by hostility

  b. ☐ showing a lack of cooperation

  c. ☐ friendly

  d. ☐ entirely cooperative

  e. ☐ disposed to be silent

4. Until then, a **minuscule** portion of his scholarly work was devoted to study of Carlyle's early writings.

  a. ☐ moderate

  b. ☐ very small

   c. ☐ major

   d. ☐ significant

   e. ☐ carefully controlled

5. Of course, how **mutable** her attitude will prove to be is unknown at this time.

   a. ☐ open to discussion

   b. ☐ firm

   c. ☐ helpful

   d. ☐ prone to change

   e. ☐ unhelpful

6. Portrayal of the artist as a **misogynist** was neither fair nor accurate.

   a. ☐ man who pursues relationships with women

   b. ☐ person who portrays women unfavorably

   c. ☐ person who hates all women

   d. ☐ effeminate man

   e. ☐ man who shows little understanding of women

7. He subsequently added more than one beautiful **seidel** to his collection.

   a. ☐ large beer glass

   b. ☐ earthenware figure

   c. ☐ primitive icon

   d. ☐ Lutheran altarpiece

   e. ☐ embroidered napkin

8. The **rubefacient** agent was ultimately shown to have had little effect.

   a. ☐ intended to soothe

   b. ☐ reducing irritation

c. ☐ intended to prevent infection

d. ☐ causing redness

e. ☐ causing roughness

9. The young monks worked hard to reach **satori.**

   a. ☐ belief that human mistakes result in human doom

   b. ☐ belief that all existence is suffering

   c. ☐ belief that the cause of suffering is desire

   d. ☐ belief that freedom from suffering is achieved by ethical conduct

   e. ☐ sudden enlightenment

10. Experts in **savate** put on exhibitions for tourists, who were delighted to pay for the privilege.

   a. ☐ form of boxing in which fists and feet are used

   b. ☐ system of memorization enabling immediate recall of complex sequences of words and numbers

   c. ☐ extraordinary ability to withstand pain

   d. ☐ extraordinary ability to pull or lift heavy weights

   e. ☐ ability to remain submerged in water for extended periods of time

■ *ZINGERS*

A. **selvage:**

   a. ☐ saving and use of waste materials

   b. ☐ edge of cloth finished to prevent unraveling

   c. ☐ protection of personal property

   d. ☐ predicted shelf life of materials susceptible to degradation

   e. ☐ morbid internalization of feelings and concerns

B. **serry:**

a. ☐ dapple
b. ☐ dry partially
c. ☐ tint
d. ☐ crowd together
e. ☐ make tooth marks

Test
NINETY

1. In this case no attempt should be made to **expunge** damaging information from employment records.

a. ☐ make public
b. ☐ explore
c. ☐ remove
d. ☐ exploit
e. ☐ explain

2. The **macabre** stories she wrote seem to have endless fascination for modern readers.

a. ☐ gruesome
b. ☐ gripping
c. ☐ romantic
d. ☐ dwelling on the supernatural
e. ☐ relating to mother love

3. Clearly, his recital of the late president's actions in that emergency was nothing less than an expertly crafted **paean.**

a. ☐ sordid account
b. ☐ attempt to deflect criticism

c. ☐   song of praise

d. ☐   attempt to destroy a reputation

e. ☐   attempt to lay blame

4. His **jocose** responses to most questions resulted in public expressions of outrage.

a. ☐   inappropriate

b. ☐   offensive

c. ☐   ill-tempered

d. ☐   ill-advised

e. ☐   joking

5. The statements are filled with **euphemisms** that do little to clarify the party's present intentions.

a. ☐   transparently feeble excuses

b. ☐   indirect expressions used in place of blunt ones

c. ☐   language deliberately chosen to make meanings obscure

d. ☐   false accounts of actions to be taken

e. ☐   ambiguous responses to questions raised by others

6. Susan rapidly became known on campus as our department's outstanding expert in **forensics.**

a. ☐   computerized medical diagnosis

b. ☐   criminal law

c. ☐   public administration

d. ☐   art of argumentation

e. ☐   religious and ethical studies

7. I know of no one who can **fulminate** as effectively as he.

a. ☐   obscure facts

b. ☐   convince members of an audience

c. ☐   present facts logically and clearly

d. ☐ express censure forcefully

e. ☐ dispute assertions of opponents

8. He proudly displayed his ancestor's **escutcheon** on a wall in the entrance hall.

a. ☐ shield bearing a coat of arms

b. ☐ ceremonial sword

c. ☐ royal document bestowing ownership of land

d. ☐ proof of noble descent

e. ☐ battle-ax

9. The physician was quick to point out that the **fontanel** had not been damaged.

a. ☐ mucous membrane lining an organ of the body

b. ☐ tube connecting organs of the body

c. ☐ small sac between a tendon and a bone

d. ☐ wall of a body cavity

e. ☐ membrane-covered opening between bones

10. I was treated to a splendid display of the **orgulous** scorn Ms. Nicholson reserved for those who disagreed with her in matters of taste.

a. ☐ deeply felt

b. ☐ haughty

c. ☐ frenzied

d. ☐ controlled

e. ☐ obvious

■ *ZINGERS*

A. **Mensur:** in German universities,

a. ☐   examination conducted monthly

b. ☐   student fencing duel fought with blunted weapons

c. ☐   academic ranking of students

d. ☐   system for granting tenure

e. ☐   entrance examination

B. **sangha:** Buddhist

a. ☐   invocation

b. ☐   vegetarian diet

c. ☐   monastic order

d. ☐   group meditation

e. ☐   initiation rite

Test
NINETY-ONE

1. To the astonishment of his colleagues, he appeared to regard the suggestion as a **panacea.**

a. ☐   stopgap

b. ☐   universally welcome thought

c. ☐   practical solution

d. ☐   remedy for all difficulties

e. ☐   laughable idea

2. What finally came into question was the **rectitude** of the attorney general.

a. ☐   soundness of judgment

b. ☐   professional training

c. ☐ moral goodness

d. ☐ objectivity

e. ☐ personal ambition

3. The misunderstanding grew out of the physician's decision to employ a **placebo** in treating the patient.

a. ☐ medicine given to humor, not cure

b. ☐ powerful sedative

c. ☐ potentially addictive substance

d. ☐ illegal narcotic

e. ☐ potentially lethal drug

4. Once the courts decided it was legal to **raze** the building, there was no further recourse.

a. ☐ burn down

b. ☐ reconstruct

c. ☐ remove all residents from

d. ☐ modernize

e. ☐ destroy completely

5. When workmen apply **oakum** improperly, they usually cause all manner of trouble for homeowners.

a. ☐ wooden flooring

b. ☐ hardwood pegs used in joining

c. ☐ finely ground wood shavings used as filler

d. ☐ adhesive used in joining wood

e. ☐ loose fiber used in caulking

6. **Oleaginous** plants have long been cultivated by food producers.

a. ☐ high in nutritional value

b. ☐ suitable for producing flour

c. ☐ containing oil

d. ☐ readily separated

e. ☐ inclined to stick together

7. No matter how far Leigh rose in the group, he was still looked on as a **parvenu.**

a. ☐ upstart

b. ☐ person of doubtful character

c. ☐ inadequately trained person

d. ☐ person of unsound judgment

e. ☐ outsider

8. When the facts were fully revealed, the affair was seen to be **redolent** of medieval intrigue.

a. ☐ free

b. ☐ suggestive

c. ☐ typical

d. ☐ unrepresentative

e. ☐ full

9. The old Mexican beggar wore her **rebozo** proudly.

a. ☐ dress made of sacking

b. ☐ short light cape

c. ☐ straw hat

d. ☐ long scarf

e. ☐ blanket

10. **Sarcophagous** animals manage to thrive everywhere in the world.

a. ☐ living underground

b. ☐ carnivorous

c. ☐ feeding on carrion

d. ☐ cave-dwelling

e. ☐ insectivorous

■ *ZINGERS*

A. **epicene:**

a. ☐ having characteristics of both sexes

b. ☐ given to flattery

c. ☐ mindless

d. ☐ leading a life of idleness

e. ☐ inordinately occupied with dress and manners

B. **hispid:**

a. ☐ sibilant

b. ☐ weblike

c. ☐ bristly

d. ☐ slurring

e. ☐ clear

Test
NINETY-TWO

1. Some historians think **megalomania** accounted for the king's behavior.

a. ☐ mental disorder marked by exaggerated feelings of poor self-esteem

b. ☐ mental disorder marked by exaggerated feelings of personal importance

c. ☐ moodiness marked by protracted periods of silence

d. ☐ intermittent delusions of persecution

e. ☐ intentional misleading of people to achieve one's aims

2. He bore the **opprobrium** willingly, because he knew he was responsible for everything done by members of his group.

a. ☐ punishment for a criminal offense

b. ☐ great expense

c. ☐ accusation of misconduct

d. ☐ disgrace brought on by shameful conduct

e. ☐ hostile response

3. Her thorough preparation for the case covered even the **minutiae.**

a. ☐ information concerning the time in which actions were taken

b. ☐ activities of people of little importance

c. ☐ unimportant details

d. ☐ information of indirect significance

e. ☐ motivations of people in a lawsuit

4. What we fail to recognize in our discussion is the fact that the decision is a **fait accompli.**

a. ☐ disagreeable private act not generally discussed in public

b. ☐ revelation made for the first time in the press

c. ☐ clear instance of personal courage

d. ☐ feat of great skill

e. ☐ thing done and past arguing against

5. The **lilliputian** furniture undoubtedly was difficult to construct.

a. ☐ extraordinarily fine

b. ☐ designed down to the smallest detail

c. ☐ tiny

d. ☐   intended for giants

e. ☐   intended for royalty

6. Friends affectionately recalled the young woman as **feisty** even on the night before her untimely death.

a. ☐   helpful

b. ☐   easy to get along with

c. ☐   undemanding

d. ☐   deeply interested in others

e. ☐   aggressive

7. The operation under discussion was performed on her **nether** lip.

a. ☐   lower

b. ☐   protruding

c. ☐   upper

d. ☐   receding

e. ☐   injured

8. Much to Alfredo's regret, from then on, **farinaceous** dishes were excluded from his diet.

a. ☐   starchy

b. ☐   fattening

c. ☐   prepared with salt

d. ☐   fried in fat

e. ☐   highly seasoned

9. A **scarab** was the only memorable item found during the extensive search conducted by the archaeologists.

a. ☐   mummy wrapping showing evidence of scarring of the corpse

b. ☐   carving of a beetle for use as a charm

c. ☐   tool used for scraping skin

d. ☐   bone fragment showing damage inflicted by blow of a weapon

e. ☐   fossil remains of a lost animal species

10. Ray misfiled the list of **nonce** words he had been collecting for many years.

a. ☐   deliberately ambiguous

b. ☐   intended to convey negative meaning

c. ☐   carrying meaning not conveyed by any other single word

d. ☐   coined for one occasion

e. ☐   containing nine letters

■   *ZINGERS*

A. **sequestrum:**

a. ☐   secure hiding place

b. ☐   piece of dead bone lying within sound bone

c. ☐   object intended to be concealed

d. ☐   animal tissue containing microorganisms

e. ☐   sum of money set aside for later use

B. **grilse:**

a. ☐   ground gray stone used as paint pigment

b. ☐   stew made of discarded foodstuffs

c. ☐   unsupported evidence introduced at a trial

d. ☐   mature salmon going to spawning grounds for the first time

e. ☐   metallic slag made usable by reprocessing

Test
NINETY-THREE

1. I wish she were not so quick to **twit** her students.

   a. ☐   criticize

   b. ☐   taunt good-humoredly

   c. ☐   correct

   d. ☐   silence

   e. ☐   condemn

2. The children said they were in favor of installing a **casement.**

   a. ☐   attic fan

   b. ☐   window fan

   c. ☐   window that opens at the side

   d. ☐   ceiling fan

   e. ☐   playroom

3. What I found myself waiting for was the exceptional **coda** I had come to know so well.

   a. ☐   striking oratorical response

   b. ☐   flambéed dessert

   c. ☐   summary of a speaker's remarks

   d. ☐   rebuttal of a lawyer's argument

   e. ☐   concluding separate section of a musical composition

4. There is no way to tell from the fossil remains whether the creature was a **ruminant.**

   a. ☐   animal that chews its cud

   b. ☐   carnivore

   c. ☐   animal of high intelligence

   d. ☐   herbivore

   e. ☐   animal that suckles its young

5. As far as I am concerned, the **trenchant** remarks I heard on that occasion have never been surpassed.

a. ☐ bitter

b. ☐ marked by lack of sympathy

c. ☐ misguided

d. ☐ strong and effective

e. ☐ marked by cruelty

6. After just a few minutes of walking along the beautiful **sward,** I found my anger beginning to leave me.

a. ☐ turf

b. ☐ rocky beach

c. ☐ lakefront

d. ☐ grand boulevard

e. ☐ high cliff

7. Much remains to be learned about the treatment of **tinnitus.**

a. ☐ inflammation of a vein

b. ☐ ringing in the ears

c. ☐ tennis elbow

d. ☐ difficulty in digesting milk

e. ☐ hardening of the cornea

8. That form of the **doxology** is entirely new to me.

a. ☐ opening prayer

b. ☐ concluding prayer

c. ☐ reading of the Gospel

d. ☐ liturgical expression of praise to God

e. ☐ invocation in a Protestant church service

9. **Diurnal** feeding is not common in that species.

   a. ☐   continual

   b. ☐   solitary

   c. ☐   occurring in daytime

   d. ☐   occurring at night

   e. ☐   performed in groups

10. The point she intends to make is that the agency acted **ultra vires** in establishing its system of penalties.

   a. ☐   with excessive haste

   b. ☐   without authorization

   c. ☐   without regard for consequences

   d. ☐   carelessly

   e. ☐   beyond legal authority

■ *ZINGERS*

A. **netsuke:** carved ornament worn with a kimono to

   a. ☐   hold the front of the robe together

   b. ☐   decorate the hair of the wearer

   c. ☐   suspend articles from a sash

   d. ☐   indicate social status of the wearer

   e. ☐   keep a sleeve in place

B. **tumpline:** line

   a. ☐   used for securing a bale of hay

   b. ☐   run around the waist for suspending tools

   c. ☐   run over the forehead to help in supporting a pack on the back

   d. ☐   used to assist in mountain climbing

   e. ☐   used for fastening a vessel to its mooring

Test
NINETY-FOUR

1. His clearest recollection is that there was no **reveille** on weekends.

   a. ☐ soldier's work schedule

   b. ☐ bugle call to get up in the morning

   c. ☐ prescribed time for going to bed

   d. ☐ military parade

   e. ☐ inspection of soldiers' barracks

2. Their **torturous** descent from the summit will never be forgotten.

   a. ☐ highly dangerous

   b. ☐ cruelly painful

   c. ☐ marked by twists and turns

   d. ☐ marked by slipping and sliding

   e. ☐ marked by starting and stopping

3. According to two neighbors, she tried more than once to **throttle** her husband.

   a. ☐ beat

   b. ☐ forgive

   c. ☐ persuade

   d. ☐ seek forgiveness of

   e. ☐ choke

4. Everyone expressed surprise over her **unseemly** behavior.

   a. ☐ marked by ingratitude

   b. ☐ thoughtless

   c. ☐ inappropriate

d. ☐   incomprehensible

e. ☐   hostile

5. Cynthia found herself unable to complete the **redaction** on schedule.

a. ☐   transfer

b. ☐   editing

c. ☐   translation

d. ☐   audit

e. ☐   authorization

6. From then on, he never went anywhere without his **truncheon.**

a. ☐   billy club

b. ☐   dog trained to attack

c. ☐   portable oxygen tank

d. ☐   trusted attendant

e. ☐   small pistol

7. My gift must not be construed as a **votive** offering.

a. ☐   expressing subservience

b. ☐   expressing agreement

c. ☐   expressing disagreement

d. ☐   expressing a vow

e. ☐   expressing sympathy

8. One of the items they looked for while out shopping was a blue **toque.**

a. ☐   artist's smock

b. ☐   embroidered handbag

c. ☐   woman's half-slip

d. ☐ woman's brimless and close-fitting hat

e. ☐ long scarf made of feathers

9. Readers may express dismay over his **turgid** language, but they go on buying his books.

a. ☐ terse

b. ☐ lacking in color

c. ☐ bombastic

d. ☐ deliberately made obscure

e. ☐ off-color

10. To my knowledge, no one has ever said he is a **whiffler.**

a. ☐ person given to evasion in argument

b. ☐ person given to self-doubt

c. ☐ person who ignores the feelings of others

d. ☐ person who expresses himself poorly

e. ☐ person who pretends ignorance of a matter concerning which he has ample knowledge

■ *ZINGERS*

A. **syce:** Indian

a. ☐ junior military officer

b. ☐ stable hand

c. ☐ instructor in a secondary school

d. ☐ holy man

e. ☐ beggar

B. **dacoit:** Indian or Burmese

a. ☐ porter assisting mountain climbers

b. ☐ village police officer

    c. ☐ instructor in marksmanship

    d. ☐ expert tracker

    e. ☐ member of a gang of armed robbers

Test
NINETY-FIVE

1. In Lee's most recent article, he lived up to his reputation as past master of **redundancy.**

    a. ☐ unclear expression

    b. ☐ forceful expression

    c. ☐ art of dodging questions

    d. ☐ recounting of inappropriate anecdotes

    e. ☐ superfluous repetition

2. We could see that **mundane** matters no longer interested her.

    a. ☐ financial

    b. ☐ economic

    c. ☐ ecclesiastical

    d. ☐ routine

    e. ☐ wide-reaching

3. I feel impelled to suggest that the explanation you offer will **redound** to your advantage.

    a. ☐ result in contributing

    b. ☐ be assumed to be

    c. ☐ not be helpful

    d. ☐ be overlooked

    e. ☐ be considered harmful

4. In the end, I must **reprehend** him for the actions he took.

 a. ☐ compliment

 b. ☐ engage in discussions with

 c. ☐ find fault with

 d. ☐ question

 e. ☐ evaluate

5. Once again we see evidence of widespread belief in **necromancy.**

 a. ☐ witchcraft

 b. ☐ communication with creatures from outer space

 c. ☐ prediction of future events based on astrological evidence

 d. ☐ ability to bring corpses back to life

 e. ☐ ability to heal the sick by unconventional means

6. It was clear from the start we once again would be treated to **mummery.**

 a. ☐ obstinate refusal to enter into frank discussion

 b. ☐ deception by artful presentation of half-truths

 c. ☐ open warfare

 d. ☐ hypocritical performance

 e. ☐ sleight of hand

7. Examination of the family photographs showed him little could be learned from examining the **lineaments** of his ancestors.

 a. ☐ family resemblances

 b. ☐ facial features

 c. ☐ female members

 d. ☐ male members

 e. ☐ appearances as indicators of personality traits

8. Once again we heard him describe all comparisons as **invidious.**

a. ☐ inept

b. ☐ resulting from envy

c. ☐ unproductive

d. ☐ unfair

e. ☐ likely to give offense

9. The party ventured into the **névé** just after dawn.

a. ☐ field of granular snow

b. ☐ shallow pond

c. ☐ rock cleft

d. ☐ vineyard

e. ☐ hidden valley

10. He resolved at that point to meet his **ineluctable** destiny head-on.

a. ☐ cruel

b. ☐ incomprehensible

c. ☐ inescapable

d. ☐ unfortunate

e. ☐ difficult

■ *ZINGERS*

A. **tenter:**

a. ☐ medieval torture rack

b. ☐ frame for drying and stretching cloth

c. ☐ hook used in deep-sea fishing

d. ☐ mallet used to pound cuts of meat

e. ☐ tool used to make patterns in fresh concrete

B. **tesselate:**

a. ☐   form into curves

b. ☐   bake at very high temperatures

c. ☐   prepare for printing

d. ☐   decorate with mosaic

e. ☐   inscribe

Test
NINETY-SIX

1. What attracted me initially was her **unaffected** manner.

a. ☐   genuine

b. ☐   earnest

c. ☐   composed

d. ☐   sympathetic

e. ☐   concerned

2. Jonathan's **earthy** humor went down well with most of the people at the dinner.

a. ☐   spontaneous

b. ☐   free of malice

c. ☐   coarse

d. ☐   honest

e. ☐   realistic

3. In light of what you have told us, we must consider Rudy **unfledged.**

a. ☐   untarnished in reputation

b. ☐   educationally unqualified

c. ☐   uncooperative

    d. ☐   lacking in personal qualities

    e. ☐   inexperienced

4. Despite decades of effort by researchers, the disease is still **pandemic.**

    a. ☐   threatening to life

    b. ☐   resistant to control

    c. ☐   spreading

    d. ☐   prevalent over a very wide area or everywhere

    e. ☐   difficult to diagnose

5. Notwithstanding his considerable success, he apparently feels it necessary to **pander** to the poor taste of his audience.

    a. ☐   offer objection

    b. ☐   minister

    c. ☐   attempt to improve

    d. ☐   call attention to

    e. ☐   refuse to adjust

6. Edith has to complete a great deal of training before she can be employed as an **actuary.**

    a. ☐   designer of sets for the stage

    b. ☐   certified public accountant

    c. ☐   expert in calculating insurance premiums

    d. ☐   social worker

    e. ☐   attorney specializing in cases involving civil rights

7. Everyone in the regiment is required to wear a **shako** in formal parades.

    a. ☐   ornamental sword in an enameled scabbard

    b. ☐   military full-dress outer coat

    c. ☐   stiff military hat with high crown and plume

d. ☐ bandolier

e. ☐ regimental sleeve emblem

8. The **billingsgate** we heard from the candidate took us completely by surprise.

a. ☐ abuse

b. ☐ nonsense

c. ☐ obvious lie

d. ☐ evasive remark

e. ☐ accusation

9. It turned out that what he had observed were **sessile** polyps.

a. ☐ consisting of seven parts

b. ☐ inhabiting the ocean depths

c. ☐ dangerous

d. ☐ immobile

e. ☐ found in the lower digestive tract

10. Basic to their teaching is the belief that God is **immanent** in nature.

a. ☐ mysteriously active

b. ☐ identifiable

c. ☐ preeminent

d. ☐ beyond understanding

e. ☐ actually present

■ *ZINGERS*

A. **semiotics:** branch of linguistics concerned with

a. ☐ signs and symbols

b. ☐ language as a system of interrelated elements

    c. ☐   the relation between use of language and the backgrounds of speakers and listeners

    d. ☐   language in its social context

    e. ☐   origins of language

B. **taiga:**

    a. ☐   rice paddy cultivator

    b. ☐   rural Indian tax collector

    c. ☐   rail around the stern of a vessel

    d. ☐   fencing thrust

    e. ☐   subarctic coniferous forest

Test
NINETY-SEVEN

1. It was the same old **shillelagh** my father brought from Ireland.

    a. ☐   woolen cap with tight headband

    b. ☐   china teapot

    c. ☐   short heavy club

    d. ☐   sword

    e. ☐   horse blanket

2. After two weeks' study of **taxidermy,** Ellen knew she had found her life's work.

    a. ☐   art of preparing, stuffing, and mounting animal skins

    b. ☐   preparation of human bodies for burial

    c. ☐   decorative preparation of food

    d. ☐   preparation of tissue for microscopic examination

    e. ☐   chemical analysis of body fluids

3. They regard animal experimentation as brutality committed under the **aegis** of scientific research.

   a. ☐   disguise

   b. ☐   stated requirement

   c. ☐   rule

   d. ☐   sponsorship

   e. ☐   pretense

4. I fully understand the **denotation** of the word, but I want to know more.

   a. ☐   implied meaning

   b. ☐   direct specific meaning

   c. ☐   recommended spelling

   d. ☐   generally accepted history

   e. ☐   intended use

5. The press reports that **oncologists** are making important advances.

   a. ☐   specialists in the study of disease

   b. ☐   specialists in the treatment of disease

   c. ☐   specialists in the use of radiant energy to diagnose and treat disease

   d. ☐   specialists in the treatment of headache

   e. ☐   specialists in the study of tumors

6. Most of us were anything but surprised when we found out he intended to **abnegate** his faith in Sunday's sermon.

   a. ☐   challenge

   b. ☐   renounce

   c. ☐   openly question

   d. ☐   remove all doubt of

   e. ☐   reaffirm

7. A researcher who depends on **serendipity** cannot anticipate consistent success.

   a. ☐   pure luck

   b. ☐   sudden insight that leads to understanding of a difficult problem

   c. ☐   self-composure under trying circumstances

   d. ☐   persistent effort in the face of repeated failure

   e. ☐   the faculty of making valuable but unexpected and accidental discoveries

8. Many connoisseurs attending the auction considered the **shoji** a choice item that would bring a record price.

   a. ☐   Japanese erotic drawing

   b. ☐   Japanese military uniform for formal occasions

   c. ☐   imperial Japanese headdress

   d. ☐   Japanese screen serving as a wall or door

   e. ☐   vertical Japanese scroll

9. As is their weekend practice, they took **tiffin** in the small room that opens onto the veranda.

   a. ☐   light midday meal

   b. ☐   afternoon tea

   c. ☐   drinks before a meal

   d. ☐   tea or coffee drunk after dinner

   e. ☐   breakfast

10. Gwen's **cattleyas** became one of her principal interests during the years she lived alone.

   a. ☐   plants of the cactus family

   b. ☐   plants of the orchid family

   c. ☐   cowslips

d. ☐   plants of the heath family

e. ☐   miniature roses

■   *ZINGERS*

A. **teratogenic:**

a. ☐   tending to produce monstrosities

b. ☐   resulting from geologic processes

c. ☐   resulting from fear

d. ☐   caused by exposure to soil particles

e. ☐   causing excessive sensitivity

B. **pica:**

a. ☐   activity intended to lure an animal into a trap

b. ☐   craving for substances other than normal food

c. ☐   reduction of anxiety by blaming others

d. ☐   prefatory remark

e. ☐   exaggeration of emotions to gain sympathy

Test
NINETY-EIGHT

1. We spent a great deal of time studying the construction of the **fronton.**

a. ☐   porch of a beach house

b. ☐   base supporting a stone monument

c. ☐   jai alai arena

d. ☐   medieval cloister

e. ☐   antechamber

2. I have been advised to **eschew** protein-rich foods.

a. ☐ emphasize
b. ☐ abstain from
c. ☐ limit the intake of
d. ☐ eat the correct proportion of
e. ☐ increase the intake of

3. When I finally understood the offer completely, I had no choice but to **demur.**

a. ☐ ask for a delay
b. ☐ indicate willingness to join in
c. ☐ offer to invest funds
d. ☐ raise objections
e. ☐ express admiration

4. Her first assignment was to **explicate** the text.

a. ☐ explain in detail
b. ☐ remove offensive words from
c. ☐ revise thoroughly
d. ☐ gain an understanding of
e. ☐ compare with an authoritative version of

5. The misrepresentation of the **cincture** was the only mistake he made in sketching the priestly vestment.

a. ☐ sleeveless outer garment
b. ☐ hood
c. ☐ shoulder decoration
d. ☐ full-length sleeve
e. ☐ belt

6. Strict construction became the party's **shibboleth** in campaigning for judicial nominees.

  a. ☐ goal

  b. ☐ slogan

  c. ☐ principal concern

  d. ☐ declared purpose

  e. ☐ hidden motive

7. After much testing, the panel decided to recommend **frangipani** as its first choice.

  a. ☐ whole wheat flour

  b. ☐ mixture of flavorings

  c. ☐ jasmine-scented perfume

  d. ☐ pale yellow

  e. ☐ colorfully printed cloth

8. In the dead days of winter, the **carapace** sat on Rebecca's shelf, serving as a reminder of the summer's field trips.

  a. ☐ species of butterfly

  b. ☐ skin of a snake

  c. ☐ ant colony

  d. ☐ hornet's nest

  e. ☐ upper shell of a turtle

9. We are certain **remanent** magnetism will be sufficient for operating the device.

  a. ☐ induced by current flow

  b. ☐ residual

  c. ☐ existing as a permanent characteristic

  d. ☐ present at the start

  e. ☐ gradually decreasing

10. Yet another three days of **fustian** await members of the society gathered in annual convention.

a. ☐   pretentious and trite writing or speech

b. ☐   lengthy debate of trivial matters

c. ☐   bitter wrangling over procedural questions

d. ☐   complete deadlock

e. ☐   inconclusive argumentation

■   *ZINGERS*

A. **fustigate:**

a. ☐   make much of minor matters

b. ☐   allow to decay

c. ☐   criticize severely

d. ☐   misuse

e. ☐   give off objectionable odors

B. **iatrogenic:**

a. ☐   resulting in abnormal fetal development

b. ☐   affecting skeletal development

c. ☐   caused by medical examination or treatment

d. ☐   arising from unknown causes

e. ☐   influenced by environmental conditions

Test
NINETY-NINE

1. His idea of elegance in dining is to serve a **gherkin** alongside an overcooked hamburger.

    a. ☐   cocktail onion

    b. ☐   portion of fried onions

    c. ☐   small cucumber used for pickling

    d. ☐   slice of hard-boiled egg

    e. ☐   small dish of relish

2. The answer he made can be described most charitably as **equivocal.**

    a. ☐   appearing to be true

    b. ☐   awaiting verification

    c. ☐   well intended

    d. ☐   ambiguous

    e. ☐   fair to all parties

3. To my surprise, her only response to my greeting was to **glower** at me.

    a. ☐   regard indifferently

    b. ☐   gaze in complete surprise

    c. ☐   stare with sullen annoyance

    d. ☐   look tenderly

    e. ☐   look questioningly

4. One of the child's teachers suggested that we have him tested for **amentia.**

    a. ☐   congenital mental deficiency

    b. ☐   visual impairment

    c. ☐   behavioral disorder

    d. ☐   thyroid malfunction

    e. ☐   pituitary malfunction

5. From the time he had that encounter with the police, his father treated him as a **wastrel.**

    a. ☐   petty thief

    b. ☐   convicted criminal

    c. ☐   person deserving of pity

    d. ☐   person lacking in judgment

    e. ☐   good-for-nothing

6. Everyone expected that the **concordat** would produce an end to the long-standing hostility.

    a. ☐   meeting of parties to a dispute

    b. ☐   agreement between church and state

    c. ☐   diplomatic mission

    d. ☐   person or agency acting as mediator

    e. ☐   stipulation

7. The veterinarian told us that all signs appeared to confirm her suspicion that the household pet was indeed **gravid.**

    a. ☐   seriously ill

    b. ☐   infectious

    c. ☐   undernourished

    d. ☐   neurologically impaired

    e. ☐   pregnant

8. The physician assured me that a **diuretic** would soon relieve my discomfort.

    a. ☐   medicine intended to be taken daily

    b. ☐   sedative

    c. ☐   drug that facilitates the flow of blood

d. ☐ substance that increases the excretion of urine

e. ☐ liver extract

9. At the banquet given in Juliet's honor, the principal speaker delivered a memorable **encomium.**

a. ☐ formal expression of high praise

b. ☐ farewell speech

c. ☐ summary of a person's achievements

d. ☐ formal address rich in classical metaphor

e. ☐ address delivered in Latin

10. She is one of a small number of women who earn their livings as **farriers.**

a. ☐ cross-country runners

b. ☐ labor mediators

c. ☐ blacksmiths who shoe horses

d. ☐ stone masons

e. ☐ common laborers

■ *ZINGERS*

A. **caza:** Turkish

a. ☐ tobacco processing plant

b. ☐ principal teacher in a village school

c. ☐ upland region

d. ☐ district administered by a judge

e. ☐ water pipe

B. **sparge:**

a. ☐ spray

b. ☐ speak ill of

c. ☐   fix in size

d. ☐   ignite intermittently

e. ☐   reverse direction of

Test
ONE HUNDRED

1. My father thought his **pince-nez** gave him a certain dignity.

a. ☐   overcoat with velvet collar

b. ☐   stiff felt hat with dome-shaped crown

c. ☐   walking stick

d. ☐   man's furled black umbrella intended to be carried in all weather

e. ☐   eyeglasses held on the nose by a spring

2. The psychologist portrayed the defendant as a **satyr,** totally unaware of the harm he brought others.

a. ☐   lustful man

b. ☐   person incapable of telling right from wrong

c. ☐   highly introverted person

d. ☐   uncontrollable rapist

e. ☐   self-professed messiah

3. By the time the annual meeting neared its end, most observers agreed that a **schism** was inevitable.

a. ☐   deadlock

b. ☐   call for an emergency meeting of directors

c. ☐   division into mutually opposed parties

d. ☐   formal dissolution of an organization

e. ☐   defiance of authority

4. Gary surely will recover from the mild depression that commonly accompanies a first experience with **unrequited** love.

   a. ☐ felt temporarily
   b. ☐ deeply felt
   c. ☐ incompletely thought out
   d. ☐ not returned
   e. ☐ unaccompanied by sexual desire

5. Johnson is frequently cited as an example of a **patronymic.**

   a. ☐ family name derived from a first name
   b. ☐ name derived from the name of a father or ancestor
   c. ☐ name derived from a place name
   d. ☐ name derived from an occupation
   e. ☐ name derived from the name of a distinguished ancestor

6. As often is the case, all of us knew Frank was a **cuckold** long before he became aware of the fact.

   a. ☐ complete fool in business matters
   b. ☐ husband of an unfaithful woman
   c. ☐ failure in a profession
   d. ☐ person afflicted with an incurable disease
   e. ☐ person who is easily taken in

7. Teachers of literature disagree with the assertion that Hemingway's style is **pellucid.**

   a. ☐ psychologically perceptive
   b. ☐ unusually interesting
   c. ☐ clear in meaning
   d. ☐ marked by lack of descriptive language
   e. ☐ marked by use of common words

8. The last thing our club needed was another **pooh-bah.**

   a. ☐   person given to insincere praise

   b. ☐   person given to excessive argumentation

   c. ☐   yes-man

   d. ☐   person who deliberately interrupts proceedings

   e. ☐   self-important person

9. Emily's **stertorous** breathing so alarmed her sister that she called a physician.

   a. ☐   making sounds resembling snoring

   b. ☐   displacing comparatively little air

   c. ☐   occurring irregularly

   d. ☐   making sounds resembling whistling

   e. ☐   occurring infrequently

10. She knew **stenosis** was causing the difficulty but could not pinpoint its location.

   a. ☐   dilation of a blood vessel

   b. ☐   weakening of the wall of a blood vessel

   c. ☐   constriction of a passage in the body

   d. ☐   rupture of a body tissue or membrane

   e. ☐   clogging of a passage in a lung

   ■ *ZINGERS*

A. **champlevé:**

   a. ☐   ritual dance performed at a burial

   b. ☐   séance held to summon departed spirits

   c. ☐   high grassy plateau

d. ☐ earthen embankment constructed to hold back water

e. ☐ enamel work with surface depressions filled with enamel colors

B. **stercoraceous:**

a. ☐ feeding on dead flesh

b. ☐ fiercely determined

c. ☐ excessively grand

d. ☐ living in or produced by dung

e. ☐ inordinately proud

ANSWER KEY

Test One	Test Two	Test Three	Test Four
1. d	1. b	1. c	1. b
2. b	2. a	2. d	2. b
3. a	3. e	3. d	3. c
4. e	4. b	4. c	4. a
5. b	5. b	5. e	5. a
6. e	6. b	6. a	6. a
7. a	7. d	7. b	7. a
8. d	8. b	8. c	8. e
9. a	9. e	9. c	9. b
10. d	10. e	10. d	10. e
■	■	■	■
A. e	A. c	A. b	A. a
B. a	B. d	B. b	B. d

Test Five	Test Six	Test Seven	Test Eight
1. c	1. c	1. c	1. a
2. a	2. a	2. b	2. d
3. e	3. e	3. e	3. c
4. b	4. b	4. b	4. b
5. d	5. e	5. a	5. e
6. c	6. c	6. c	6. b
7. b	7. b	7. d	7. d
8. a	8. a	8. b	8. e
9. e	9. d	9. a	9. c
10. b	10. d	10. e	10. a
■	■	■	■
A. c	A. b	A. b	A. b
B. a	B. c	B. d	B. e

ANSWER KEY

Test Nine	Test Ten	Test Eleven	Test Twelve
1. c	1. b	1. d	1. a
2. a	2. c	2. c	2. b
3. e	3. e	3. a	3. c
4. c	4. b	4. d	4. b
5. d	5. a	5. b	5. d
6. e	6. d	6. e	6. e
7. a	7. a	7. a	7. c
8. b	8. c	8. c	8. a
9. d	9. e	9. b	9. a
10. b	10. b	10. a	10. b
■	■	■	■
A. c	A. d	A. b	A. d
B. a	B. c	B. e	B. c

Test Thirteen	Test Fourteen	Test Fifteen	Test Sixteen
1. e	1. b	1. a	1. c
2. b	2. d	2. c	2. a
3. d	3. e	3. e	3. a
4. c	4. a	4. d	4. b
5. a	5. e	5. b	5. c
6. c	6. b	6. a	6. d
7. b	7. c	7. c	7. e
8. a	8. d	8. e	8. b
9. e	9. a	9. c	9. c
10. a	10. c	10. b	10. a
■	■	■	■
A. b	A. b	A. a	A. d
B. d	B. d	B. c	B. a

Test Seventeen	Test Eighteen	Test Nineteen	Test Twenty
1. b	1. d	1. b	1. c
2. d	2. a	2. c	2. c
3. a	3. b	3. e	3. e
4. e	4. a	4. b	4. b
5. a	5. c	5. a	5. a
6. c	6. b	6. d	6. d
7. c	7. d	7. e	7. e
8. e	8. b	8. b	8. b
9. b	9. e	9. c	9. a
10. c	10. a	10. a	10. c
■	■	■	■
A. b	A. c	A. b	A. c
B. d	B. c	B. d	B. a

330

Test Twenty-one	Test Twenty-two	Test Twenty-three	Test Twenty-four
1. e	1. b	1. a	1. d
2. a	2. c	2. b	2. c
3. c	3. e	3. c	3. b
4. d	4. b	4. b	4. a
5. a	5. a	5. a	5. b
6. e	6. c	6. e	6. e
7. b	7. d	7. d	7. a
8. b	8. e	8. c	8. c
9. c	9. b	9. a	9. b
10. a	10. c	10. e	10. c
■	■	■	■
A. c	A. d	A. b	A. e
B. a	B. a	B. b	B. a

Test Twenty-five	Test Twenty-six	Test Twenty-seven	Test Twenty-eight
1. a	1. b	1. e	1. a
2. b	2. c	2. c	2. c
3. d	3. d	3. b	3. e
4. c	4. d	4. d	4. c
5. c	5. a	5. c	5. b
6. e	6. b	6. a	6. d
7. a	7. c	7. b	7. a
8. c	8. b	8. a	8. a
9. e	9. d	9. c	9. b
10. b	10. a	10. b	10. b
■	■	■	■
A. c	A. b	A. d	A. c
B. b	B. e	B. a	B. b

Test Twenty-nine	Test Thirty	Test Thirty-one	Test Thirty-two
1. c	1. b	1. a	1. b
2. d	2. a	2. c	2. c
3. b	3. d	3. a	3. d
4. a	4. e	4. d	4. a
5. d	5. c	5. b	5. a
6. c	6. d	6. e	6. c
7. b	7. c	7. c	7. b
8. d	8. b	8. a	8. e
9. e	9. d	9. c	9. e
10. b	10. a	10. d	10. b
■	■	■	■
A. b	A. c	A. b	A. c
B. c	B. a	B. e	B. d

Test Thirty-three	Test Thirty-four	Test Thirty-five	Test Thirty-six
1. b	1. b	1. c	1. d
2. c	2. c	2. a	2. c
3. a	3. b	3. d	3. e
4. c	4. a	4. c	4. d
5. c	5. d	5. e	5. a
6. d	6. d	6. b	6. e
7. b	7. e	7. a	7. b
8. a	8. b	8. a	8. c
9. d	9. a	9. b	9. d
10. d	10. c	10. c	10. b
■	■	■	■
A. a	A. b	A. c	A. d
B. c	B. d	B. d	B. b

Test Thirty-seven	Test Thirty-eight	Test Thirty-nine	Test Forty
1. b	1. c	1. a	1. b
2. a	2. e	2. c	2. a
3. d	3. b	3. e	3. d
4. e	4. d	4. c	4. c
5. a	5. b	5. d	5. a
6. b	6. c	6. a	6. e
7. c	7. a	7. b	7. a
8. e	8. c	8. d	8. e
9. a	9. e	9. c	9. a
10. b	10. b	10. a	10. b
■	■	■	■
A. b	A. e	A. b	A. c
B. c	B. b	B. e	B. d

Test Forty-one	Test Forty-two	Test Forty-three	Test Forty-four
1. a	1. c	1. c	1. c
2. d	2. d	2. a	2. b
3. d	3. a	3. b	3. e
4. b	4. e	4. e	4. a
5. e	5. a	5. b	5. a
6. c	6. a	6. d	6. e
7. a	7. c	7. e	7. b
8. c	8. b	8. b	8. d
9. e	9. d	9. c	9. c
10. b	10. e	10. a	10. b
■	■	■	■
A. e	A. d	A. c	A. b
B. c	B. b	B. e	B. a

Test Forty-five	Test Forty-six	Test Forty-seven	Test Forty-eight
1. a	1. a	1. d	1. c
2. e	2. b	2. d	2. d
3. c	3. a	3. e	3. e
4. d	4. c	4. a	4. b
5. b	5. b	5. a	5. a
6. a	6. a	6. d	6. a
7. c	7. e	7. c	7. c
8. d	8. d	8. e	8. e
9. b	9. b	9. b	9. d
10. e	10. c	10. c	10. b
■	■	■	■
A. a	A. e	A. d	A. b
B. b	B. b	B. a	B. e

Test Forty-nine	Test Fifty	Test Fifty-one	Test Fifty-two
1. d	1. c	1. d	1. b
2. e	2. d	2. d	2. a
3. c	3. b	3. c	3. d
4. a	4. e	4. b	4. a
5. b	5. a	5. e	5. e
6. e	6. b	6. a	6. c
7. c	7. c	7. e	7. e
8. b	8. a	8. c	8. a
9. a	9. d	9. b	9. b
10. a	10. e	10. c	10. c
■	■	■	■
A. c	A. e	A. d	A. b
B. c	B. a	B. b	B. e

Test Fifty-three	Test Fifty-four	Test Fifty-five	Test Fifty-six
1. a	1. e	1. a	1. c
2. c	2. c	2. d	2. e
3. c	3. b	3. e	3. d
4. e	4. a	4. e	4. a
5. b	5. b	5. c	5. b
6. d	6. a	6. a	6. d
7. a	7. d	7. b	7. b
8. b	8. d	8. d	8. c
9. d	9. e	9. c	9. e
10. c	10. b	10. b	10. c
■	■	■	■
A. d	A. b	A. a	A. a
B. a	B. c	B. d	B. d

333

ANSWER KEY

Test Fifty-seven	Test Fifty-eight	Test Fifty-nine	Test Sixty
1. a	1. a	1. e	1. c
2. c	2. c	2. a	2. b
3. a	3. b	3. b	3. d
4. d	4. e	4. d	4. e
5. e	5. d	5. e	5. a
6. d	6. c	6. a	6. b
7. b	7. b	7. c	7. c
8. c	8. a	8. b	8. d
9. e	9. d	9. d	9. e
10. b	10. e	10. c	10. b
■	■	■	■
A. d	A. a	A. e	A. b
B. e	B. c	B. d	B. e

Test Sixty-one	Test Sixty-two	Test Sixty-three	Test Sixty-four
1. e	1. d	1. e	1. c
2. c	2. e	2. b	2. b
3. b	3. a	3. d	3. e
4. a	4. c	4. a	4. a
5. e	5. c	5. c	5. c
6. e	6. a	6. e	6. d
7. c	7. b	7. d	7. b
8. a	8. d	8. c	8. e
9. b	9. e	9. b	9. a
10. d	10. b	10. d	10. d
■	■	■	■
A. a	A. c	A. c	A. d
B. d	B. a	B. e	B. a

Test Sixty-five	Test Sixty-six	Test Sixty-seven	Test Sixty-eight
1. c	1. b	1. a	1. e
2. e	2. d	2. c	2. e
3. d	3. c	3. e	3. d
4. a	4. e	4. d	4. c
5. a	5. d	5. b	5. b
6. b	6. c	6. c	6. a
7. e	7. a	7. d	7. e
8. d	8. b	8. a	8. d
9. b	9. e	9. e	9. c
10. c	10. a	10. b	10. a
■	■	■	■
A. c	A. e	A. a	A. c
B. d	B. b	B. c	B. b

Test Sixty-nine	Test Seventy	Test Seventy-one	Test Seventy-two
1. b	1. b	1. b	1. b
2. e	2. e	2. c	2. b
3. d	3. b	3. e	3. e
4. a	4. d	4. d	4. d
5. e	5. c	5. d	5. c
6. e	6. a	6. a	6. a
7. b	7. c	7. b	7. e
8. c	8. e	8. c	8. d
9. c	9. e	9. e	9. c
10. b	10. c	10. a	10. b
■	■	■	■
A. d	A. b	A. e	A. d
B. d	B. e	B. c	B. b

Test Seventy-three	Test Seventy-four	Test Seventy-five	Test Seventy-six
1. d	1. e	1. d	1. e
2. d	2. d	2. c	2. b
3. b	3. d	3. a	3. c
4. a	4. b	4. b	4. d
5. a	5. a	5. c	5. e
6. c	6. c	6. a	6. c
7. b	7. b	7. c	7. a
8. e	8. e	8. e	8. b
9. d	9. d	9. d	9. a
10. c	10. a	10. b	10. d
■	■	■	■
A. d	A. e	A. a	A. e
B. b	B. b	B. c	B. c

Test Seventy-seven	Test Seventy-eight	Test Seventy-nine	Test Eighty
1. a	1. c	1. e	1. b
2. c	2. b	2. d	2. c
3. d	3. e	3. a	3. e
4. a	4. c	4. c	4. a
5. e	5. e	5. b	5. e
6. e	6. d	6. e	6. b
7. b	7. b	7. d	7. d
8. d	8. b	8. b	8. c
9. c	9. d	9. a	9. b
10. b	10. a	10. c	10. d
■	■	■	■
A. b	A. d	A. a	A. a
B. d	B. b	B. d	B. c

ANSWER KEY

Test Eighty-one
1. d
2. a
3. b
4. e
5. c
6. d
7. a
8. a
9. c
10. b

■

A. e
B. a

Test Eighty-two
1. c
2. b
3. d
4. b
5. d
6. a
7. e
8. c
9. c
10. a

■

A. b
B. c

Test Eighty-three
1. e
2. d
3. a
4. b
5. c
6. d
7. c
8. a
9. b
10. e

■

A. c
B. a

Test Eighty-four
1. b
2. c
3. e
4. d
5. a
6. b
7. c
8. d
9. e
10. a

■

A. d
B. e

Test Eighty-five
1. b
2. c
3. e
4. c
5. d
6. d
7. e
8. a
9. c
10. b

■

A. e
B. b

Test Eighty-six
1. c
2. e
3. a
4. b
5. a
6. d
7. c
8. e
9. b
10. e

■

A. d
B. c

Test Eighty-seven
1. c
2. b
3. a
4. e
5. d
6. c
7. b
8. e
9. a
10. d

■

A. e
B. b

Test Eighty-eight
1. b
2. a
3. e
4. c
5. a
6. e
7. d
8. b
9. d
10. c

■

A. a
B. d

Test Eighty-nine
1. c
2. b
3. e
4. b
5. d
6. c
7. a
8. d
9. e
10. a

■

A. b
B. d

Test Ninety
1. c
2. a
3. c
4. e
5. b
6. d
7. d
8. a
9. e
10. b

■

A. b
B. c

Test Ninety-one
1. d
2. c
3. a
4. e
5. e
6. c
7. a
8. b
9. d
10. b

■

A. a
B. c

Test Ninety-two
1. b
2. d
3. c
4. e
5. c
6. e
7. a
8. a
9. b
10. d

■

A. b
B. d

Test Ninety-three
1. b
2. c
3. e
4. a
5. d
6. a
7. b
8. d
9. c
10. e

A. c
B. c

Test Ninety-four
1. b
2. b
3. e
4. c
5. b
6. a
7. d
8. d
9. c
10. a

A. b
B. e

Test Ninety-five
1. e
2. d
3. a
4. c
5. a
6. d
7. b
8. e
9. a
10. c

A. b
B. d

Test Ninety-six
1. a
2. c
3. e
4. d
5. b
6. c
7. c
8. a
9. d
10. e

A. a
B. e

Test Ninety-seven
1. c
2. a
3. d
4. b
5. e
6. b
7. e
8. d
9. a
10. b

A. a
B. b

Test Ninety-eight
1. c
2. b
3. d
4. a
5. e
6. b
7. c
8. e
9. b
10. a

A. c
B. c

Test Ninety-nine
1. c
2. d
3. c
4. a
5. e
6. b
7. e
8. d
9. a
10. c

A. d
B. a

Test One Hundred
1. e
2. a
3. c
4. d
5. b
6. b
7. c
8. e
9. a
10. c

A. e
B. d

INDEX OF TEST WORDS

NUMBERS IN PARENTHESES REFER TO TEST NUMBERS.

buccal (30)
bucolic (49)
bulimia (80)
bungle (68)
burgeon (16)
bursar (76)
busby (53)

C

cabal (68)
cabochon (32)
cabriole (5)
cachepot (16)
cachet (33)
cacophony (84)
caesura (26)
caldera (23)
calliope (76)
callous (9)
calumet (36)
calumny (21)
campanile (27)
canaille (32)
cant (35)
capacious (5)
caparison (25)
capitulate (33)
captious (14)
caracole (40)
carapace (98)
caries (78)
carphology (44)
carping (18)
carpophagous (43)
cartel (76)
casement (93)
castigate (1)
casuistry (37)
catafalque (31)
catharsis (28)
cattleya (97)
caul (62)
cavil (78)
caza (99)

cenacle (38)
centaur (20)
cerements (42)
chamfer (65)
champlevé (100)
chary (51)
chauvinist (15)
cheroot (31)
chrestomathy (4)
cicatrix (34)
cincture (98)
circinate (60)
clerestory (9)
clerihew (3)
cloy (36)
coalesce (13)
coda (93)
cogent (11)
cognition (56)
coif (64)
colloquy (52)
comatose (47)
compote (63)
compunction (44)
concinnity (40)
concomitant (65)
concordat (99)
confabulate (63)
conjure (58)
connotation (8)
consuetude (21)
contravene (64)
contumely (36)
corrigenda (75)
crapulous (29)
credulity (82)
creel (45)
crestfallen (52)
crewel (58)
crotchety (55)
crouton (83)
crucible (88)
cryptic (60)
cubeb (64)
cuckold (100)

cul-de-sac (42)
cummerbund (84)
cumshaw (75)
cunctation (45)
cupidity (46)
cupreous (61)
curmudgeon (53)
cursory (44)
cynosure (59)

D

dacha (32)
dacoit (94)
damson (82)
dashiki (38)
debacle (1)
decadence (33)
decorum (5)
defenestration (76)
deleterious (1)
demagogue (8)
demean (65)
demise (45)
demulcent (55)
demur (98)
denotation (97)
denouement (62)
deprecate (63)
desiccate (82)
desideratum (17)
desuetude (66)
dexterity (18)
dharma (9)
diapason (49)
diaspora (13)
diastrophism (84)
didactic (31)
diffidence (29)
dilatory (23)
dimity (64)
dingo (56)
dipterous (40)
dirge (42)
disaffected (75)

foible (26)
folderol (61)
foment (33)
fontanel (90)
fop (68)
foreboding (6)
forensics (90)
fortuitous (21)
frangible (27)
frangipani (98)
fraught (76)
frenetic (22)
friable (82)
frisson (84)
fronton (98)
froward (30)
frump (47)
fulgent (50)
fulgurate (24)
fulminate (90)
funambulist (71)
fungible (11)
furbelow (88)
fuscous (13)
fustian (98)
fustigate (98)

G

gadfly (6)
gadroon (40)
gaffe (15)
gainsay (76)
gambit (29)
gamut (13)
garrulous (59)
gauche (1)
gazebo (53)
gecko (23)
genre (46)
genuflect (75)
germane (71)
gerontocracy (41)
ghee (2)
gherkin (99)

gibbet (52)
gibe (88)
gimlet (62)
girasol (16)
glabrous (41)
glower (99)
gnosis (41)
golem (83)
gonfalon (32)
gongoristic (18)
goniometer (50)
graticule (65)
gratuitous (41)
gravamen (57)
gravid (99)
gregariousness (76)
griffin (56)
grilse (92)
grouper (87)
guano (18)
gumbo (80)

H

habitué (49)
hachure (38)
haggis (61)
hagiography (15)
hajj (30)
hakim (77)
halcyon (13)
hapax legomenon (2)
haplessness (6)
harbinger (47)
harridan (30)
haruspex (12)
hassock (71)
hauteur (59)
havelock (82)
heady (68)
hebdomadal (18)
hebetude (8)
hecatomb (71)
hegemony (14)
hegira (83)

heinous (21)
heliolatry (88)
helot (25)
helve (2)
hemiplegia (85)
henotheism (10)
heterodox (85)
heuristic (33)
hiatus (41)
hibernaculum (21)
hidrosis (36)
himation (37)
hinterlands (55)
hirsute (37)
hispid (91)
hoary (87)
hogan (42)
hoi polloi (51)
holophrastic (41)
homage (26)
homeopathy (11)
homily (63)
homogeneous (80)
homunculus (84)
honorarium (61)
hoyden (28)
humectant (9)
hussar (64)
hyperbole (16)

I

iatrogenic (98)
iconoclast (6)
iconography (84)
idiosyncrasy (49)
ignis fatuus (9)
ignominious (10)
illation (16)
illusory (68)
imago (45)
imbricate (24)
imbroglio (2)
imbue (46)
immanent (96)

immolate (13)
impasse (38)
impeachment (27)
implicit (64)
imprimatur (15)
impugn (65)
inalienable (55)
inane (23)
inanition (70)
inchoate (2)
incontinent (32)
incubus (40)
indigenous (81)
indolent (58)
ineffable (20)
ineluctable (95)
infamous (83)
infinitesimal (14)
in flagrante delicto (75)
ingenuous (17)
inglenook (81)
inherent (88)
inordinate (42)
insidious (66)
insouciance (57)
inspissate (21)
intaglio (33)
interdict (52)
internecine (10)
intestate (50)
intrados (33)
intransigent (13)
inure (47)
invidious (95)
irrefragable (11)

J

janissary (1)
jape (59)
jaundiced (64)
jejune (18)
jeremiad (6)
jeroboam (63)

jettison (46)
jocose (90)
jocular (24)
jocund (4)
jongleur (35)
joust (29)
juggernaut (36)
Junoesque (66)
juvenilia (32)

K

kakemono (34)
ketch (11)
kiosk (56)
koan (23)
kowtow (2)
krummholz (16)
kurtosis (39)

L

labile (82)
laconic (59)
lacunae (70)
lagniappe (2)
lambent (22)
languid (49)
lanuginous (6)
lapidary (58)
lapsus calami (16)
largesse (83)
lassitude (27)
lectern (32)
lenity (2)
leonine (64)
leprosarium (79)
lese majesty (33)
leviathan (26)
libertine (80)
lilliputian (92)
limpid (51)
lineaments (95)
lingua franca (79)
lissome (21)

litotes (54)
littoral (27)
loam (56)
loath (35)
locum tenens (10)
loess (38)
logomachy (19)
lordosis (81)
lubricious (7)
Luddite (43)
lugubrious (29)
lumbering (55)
lurid (79)
lusus naturae (85)
lycanthrope (81)

M

macabre (90)
macerate (56)
magnum opus (76)
mahout (71)
majuscule (78)
maladroit (2)
malapropism (6)
malinger (72)
Mammon (84)
mandible (20)
manege (41)
Manichean (13)
mansard (62)
mansuetude (3)
mantra (87)
marasmus (6)
marmoreal (24)
masticate (65)
matutinal (47)
maunder (19)
meander (72)
megalomania (92)
mélange (25)
mellifluous (45)
mendicant (37)
Mensur (90)
mensurable (42)